THE
GREENS, GRITS, & HOECAKES
COOKBOOK

*.....***soul food** *that'll knock your socks off*

by: Carolyn Buckner

© **2008 Carolyn Buckner**

Reprinted in 2018, 2021

All rights reserved. No part of this book may be reproduced or transmitted in any form or by any means, electronic or mechanical, including photocopying, recording or by any informational storage or retrieval system, except by a reviewer who may quote brief passages in a review to be printed in a magazine or newspaper-without permission in writing from the publisher.

There are a number of elements that contribute to what we know as soul food.

Its foundation is, of course, foods and methods used for hundreds of years in Africa. Those folks who came to America as slaves rather quickly changed from the rather bland African foods to high-octane versions by adding ingredients they learned about from Native Americans, and the European sharecroppers.

An interesting circumstance that influenced what the slaves ate was that they were the ones who ended up with the parts of animals the folks in the big house did not want. That was a blessing in disguise since the odd parts of animals are the most flavorful. Out of that came these delicious dishes involving chitlins, hocks, souses, cracklin's, scrapple and many more.

Small game, garden raised vegetables, and ingredients found in the wild round out that array of wonderful dishes we know as Soul Food.

ACKNOWLEDGEMENTS

I would personally like to thank all my Sisters and Brothers of Electa Grand Chapter, O.E.S., State of Iowa, P.H.A., Inc., who contributed to the success of *Our Heritage Soul Cook Book*. Many thanks for sharing your recipes as well as sharing your family remedies that have been passed down from generation to generation. These recipes and remedies tell a story that helps to keep our Black Heritage living from one generation to the next. They continue to say that we love each other, we respect each other, and that we are a proud people. Sisters and Brothers, you have made this cookbook possible.

Carolyn A. Buckner, G.W.M.
2004-2006

Any recipe in this book that involves canning should not be considered to be complete. The user of this book should consult other resources to learn the techniques and dangers involved in home canning.

Neither the writer nor the publisher will assume responsibility for loss or injury resulting from improper canning techniques.

TABLE OF CONTENTS

APPETIZERS and BEVERAGES	27
SOUPS	35
SALADS	43
BREADS	49
VEGETABLES	61
MAIN & MEAT DISHES	71
DESSERTS	99
CONDIMENTS	111
GRANDMA'S APRON	118
WASHING CLOTHES	119
ABBREVIATIONS	120
HELPFUL HINTS	121

Our Heritage groups of Afro-Americans have had a profound influence on many aspects of American culture, especially cooking. Our groups, some as slaves and some also as free men, came to America from many parts of Africa. We came carrying the memory of foods and dishes from our homeland.

As decendents of these first Afro-Americans, many traditional foods of Africa were adapted and honored so that they were no longer African dishes but Afro-American. The red bean soup, bean stews and black-eyed peas dishes have been transformed into dishes of ham hocks with black-eyed peas. The African method of cooking spinach has been adapted to Afro-American cooking of turnips, greens, kale, collards and mustard greens.

The gumbos of Africa changed from bland stews with okra to zippy American version incorporated with tomatoes and rice. In the Black Heritage, but separate from Afro-American, cooking is what is commonly called Soul Food. This type of cooking comprises not only African traditions but also the food influences of the American Indian and the European along with the sharecroppers. It developed out of limited resources of all these groups, which means it included lots of fresh vegetables, chicken, cornmeal, game and whatever parts of the hog and cow were rejected by those who could afford to be choosy. Some of the most famous Soul Foods are chitterlings, hoecakes and possum.

Some of our recipes you will find in this book have been passed down through generations by word of mouth. This is part of our legacy, and we hope you will enjoy as well as learn more about our Heritage in cooking and remedies as well as keeping our legacy alive for our next generations to follow.

>	Carolyn A. Buckner, G.W.M.
>	Osumana (Veni) Cassell, 33°, G.W.P.
>	Patricia White, G.A.M.
>	Russell J. Burt, 33°, G.A.P.
>	Marjorie Marsh, P.G.W.M. Grand Treasurer
>	Hattie M. Middleton, Grand Secretary

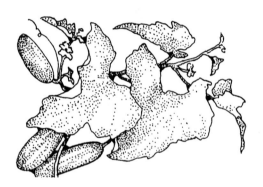

A Soul Welcome and Remembrance

In an African American home, everyone knew that a typical welcome was that you were wanted anytime. You didn't have to phone or wait for a special invitation. It was like seeing a friend- you go- and if it's mealtime, you draw up a chair and eat. You were always welcomed. There'll always be enough food because you never knew who would be dropping in just to say "hello". Everyone was family, and families were numberless. It seemed like a pot was always waiting; and this pot on the stove

gave a Soul Welcome to everyone. A Soul Welcome comes from way back in the days when we were slaves. For over 200 years, we were told where to live and where to work. We were given husbands, and we made children, and all these things could be taken away from us. The only real comfort came at the end of the day when we took either the food that we were given or the food that we raised or the food that we had caught and we put it in the pot and sat with our kin and talked, sang, and ate.

We all have special close friends; we call them "tight friends." Most of us call the mothers of our tight friends Mama because these are women who have helped raise us. We've spent as much time in their homes as in our own, and they have spanked us and loved us and patched us up so many times that they are, in a sense, our "Mamas". In our Gram's or our Nana's kitchen, there were usually no cookbooks. One would usually start with beating up biscuits; and with a hint or two from Mama, Gram, or Nana, they came out tasting just right. The men didn't say much about the cooking unless it was really bad. They just ate. The heart of the house was the kitchen.

Remember the lawn parties at the church during the summer? These were held outside and were like a small bazaar. The women would put up stands, and they'd fill them with snowballs, hot dogs, homemade cakes, homemade ice cream and pies. They'd always take out the strings of lights and put them up to make you feel as though it was an occasion. These lawn parties weren't big affairs, and I doubt whether they added much to the church treasury, but they certainly did liven up a hot summer night in the town. Remember when a friend would

shout, "Get a dime and come on over to the church." Sometime you wouldn't put your shoes on because you were going to be on the lawn of the church. If you were going inside, you'd not only have to put on shoes but your best dress, hat, and gloves. Your best clothes were always saved for church and not for parties. Those were nice nights, but they've given way to movies amusement parks, nightclubs, and television (all the things that weren't open or available to us then).

Homecoming was one of the biggest events at church, and everyone knew the date a year in advance. It was planned a year in advance so everyone could mark the date on their calendar to come back, if possible, from all over the country to the church where they were baptized. Homecoming means just that . . . coming home. The revivals and special services go on for a whole week and still do today; and in between your visit with your friends you would EAT. The men would plan the events. Now, usually the women do, and the women do the cooking the same for today's Homecoming. On the final Sunday of Homecoming, there was always a large banquet in the church and certain women were assigned to bring special dishes typical of today gathering. No woman ever entered the church empty handed the Sunday of Homecoming. By the time everyone was there, the tables were heaped high with everything that we loved to eat. A typical Homecoming menu included: fried chicken, potato salad, country ham, polish ham, barbecued ham, bake ham, cole slaw, greens, corn pudding, sweet potatoes, mashed white potatoes, biscuit, rolls, cornbread and all kinds of relishes

and preserves. The sweet tables, also known as the dessert table, usually held at least two dozen different cakes and pies. Everyone had their favorite cooks, and Homecoming was the time to ask for Sis. Nelson potato salad with her homemade salad dressing, Sis. Weldon's lemon cake, Sis. Roach's relishes and preserves, Sis. Alston's greens and Grandma Griggs's fried chicken that was thoroughly scrubbed with Ivory soap and rinsed several times before cooking. I've never seen a scrap of food go begging on the platters.

The other big yearly event is the celebration of the Church's Birthday, which is called the Church Anniversary. We follow the same schedule as Homecoming, revivals, special services, and

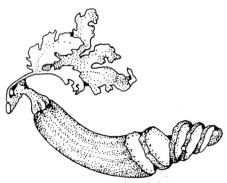

then on the actual birthday we have the banquet. The menu for the banquet doesn't change either . . . there is no need because, at both occasions, we include everything we love to eat. Not as many out-of-towners come back for the Church Anniversary; but because a large number of in town guests come, it seems as big as Homecoming. It is just as important to us, for we would never slight the church on its birthday. As a matter of fact, we never slight anyone on his or her birthday. Most of us have given ourselves birthday parties; and by the time we ask our friends and they ask their friends, you get a big talking, eating, and dancing crowd that sometimes doesn't go home until morning. A birthday party no matter what your age, every African American gives himself or herself a birthday party. It usually starts about 9 p.m. and ends when someone happens to notice that the sun is coming up. The only vital ingredient is music, but of course, a bar and a buffet are expected. A dish served depends on the mood and energy. If a birthday falls on a weekend, one could spend the day cooking and cleaning chitterlings. If it came on a weeknight, one could spend the night before frying chicken. In recent years, however we have veered away from traditional favorites.

When Afro Americans could not participate in all clubs they were great joiners. Joiners of the Masons, Order of the Eastern Star, American Legion, the Elks and to the United Order of Tents. The Tents started at the end of the Civil War as a Woman's Burial Society. If you paid fifty cents a month, the Tents would give you a fifty dollar funeral; a dollar a month got back a hundred dollar funeral, and so on. The Tents, besides

keeping up the funeral benefits sell insurance polices and even ran a old age home. Another club of interest that existed long before Christmas Clubs was called a Saving Club. They usually consisted of 20 people who set aside a certain amount of money to put in a joint saving account. They received more interest doing it this way than they would if each had separate accounts. At Christmas, they took it all out and divided it. Each month they would get together at a member's house; and although it only took five minutes to collect the money and discuss a little business, they spent the rest of the night eating. At the Saving Club meeting, the menu consisted of fried chicken, ham, potato salad, greens plus many bottles of someone's homemade specialty wine. The Saving Club then had a good reason to have a big party once a month.

Before the Red Hat Society Ladies Club existed, a club called the Luncheon Club was started by the women of the church. It consisted of about a dozen women who would get all dressed up in hats and good dresses and gloves in the middle of the day and go to a member's house for lunch. The hostess would really get away from the traditional foods. The menu always sounded like something out of the Thursday food page in the newspaper . . . creamed chicken in patty shells or crab salad with all the little decorations around it. They'd sit the dinning room table with the best linen and every piece of silver that the hostess owned.

Last, but not least, was Family Reunion as part of the Welcome. Every family likes to touch base at least once a year, especially now that so many of us have left home. Families pour in from all over the country. Everyone is put up all around the town because, even now that we can, no one wants to stay at a motel. Neighbors and friends lend their extra beds and pitch in with the cooking. When the weather is nice, and it usually is, they spread long tables outside underneath the trees and keep them filled with food from noon on. There is always new husband and wives and babies to meet, new jobs to talk about, a few of the old people to cry over. Everybody has to catch up with everybody else, and that takes at least three to four days. Keeping our Heritage alive for the next generations is so important to all of us.

A typical Christmas Buffet Menu:

Turkey with cornbread stuffing
    and giblet gravy
Smithfield Ham
Chicken
String beans
Collard Greens
Sweet Peas
Sweet Potatoes
Corn Pudding
Potato Salad
Lettuce and Tomatoes
Biscuits
Rolls

Cornbread
Cranberry Sauce
Pickles, Olives,
    Relish Homemade
Apple Pie
Pumpkin Pie
Caramel Cake
Chocolate Cake
Fruitcake
Pound Cake
Brownies
Cookies
Eggnog

The buffet is a city invention: Christmas dinner in the country means sit down with the family. The ingredients for the dinner are mainly homegrown.

Christmas Dinner in the Country:

Roast Goose or Duck with Dressing and Gravy
Roast Pork
Collard Greens or Cabbage
Mashed Potatoes or Baked Sweet Potatoes
Turnips
Plum Pudding with Hard Sauce
Homemade Cakes
Raisin Pie

Now, that I have given you the Welcome, it is time to look in the pot. Basically, our food is simple, inexpensive, and plentiful. As

slaves, our daily ration included one salt herring and one pint of cornmeal. Occasionally, a piece of salt pork was substituted for the herring. On fortunate days, we were given our milk or buttermilk and perhaps a portion of molasses. In Virginia, slaves were often allowed to raise vegetables, chickens, and a few pigs. Corn was the main garden crop because it did not require much care and could be used either as a vegetable, or

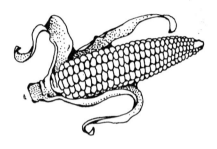

it could be ground and used for bread. Poke, dandelion and other greens were gathered wild. Every few years the pigs were turned out of their pens, and turnips were grown in the fertile soil. Variety was added to the diets with fish and crabs from the rivers and small game from the surroundings forest. The basic ingredients – Corn, Pork, Chicken, Greens, Seafood, Sour or Buttermilk and Molasses have stayed with us for 300 years plus and still form the heart of Afro Americans cooking. We've added sauces, spices, butter, relishes and wines – we've pretty much replaced molasses with sugar; and new houses have taken away most of our small game, but essentially, we still start with the same foods. The Welcome that comes from our kitchens depends on these basic six ingredients.

Remedies for a Cold

After wrapping up in a flannel gown or flannel pajamas, rub the chest to break up a cold with goose grease made from the goose grease saved from the Christmas goose. Drink some hot toddy and go to bed.

> Hot Toddy Recipe
> 1 cup hot water
> 1 teaspoon sugar
> 2 teaspoons of whiskey

Note: For Children use only a ½ jigger of whiskey.

To ward off colds for the winter, take 1 teaspoon of cod liver oil every morning in the winter. For a laxative once a week, take 1 teaspoon of castor oil in a glass of orange juice and ¼ teaspoon of baking soda; this will foam up.

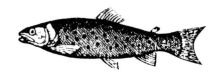

ODE TO THE DIETER

Cholesterol is poisonous. So never, never eat it.
Sugar, too, may murder you; there is no way
    to beat it.
And fatty food may do you in; be certain to avoid it.
Some food was rich in vitamins, but processing   destroyed it.
So let your life be ordered by each documented fact
And die of malnutrition – but with arteries intact.

GREENS

Some variety of greens accompanies most meals. Many of them are garden-grown, or purchased at the supermarket, but others, such as mustard, dandelion, and poke still grow wild in the area and are there for the picking. It's amazing to us to think that anyone could grow up without greens.

KALE, TURNIP, MUSTARD, COLLARD, AND CABBAGE

Cut off the big stems. Make a strong, warm, salt water solution in sink and soak the greens. This will take all the dirt and sand to the bottom. Drain this water off and rinse in clear water until no dirt or sand is seen. Drain.

If you are cooking with meat – ham hocks or ham skin – have the meat boiling while cleaning the greens. Put greens into cook with the meat. Add 1 pod of red pepper, a small whole onion, peeled, and salt to taste. Cook until greens are tender, about 1 1/2 hours for most greens. When done add a pinch of sugar or monosodium glutamate. (Some people prefer to add 1 teaspoon of sugar per pound of greens to the pot at the beginning of the cooking time to help the greens maintain their color.)

NEVER DRAIN THE GREENS. Since most of the vitamins are in the pot liquor you must make sure that some of it is spooned out with each helping. Greens are usually eaten topped with chopped, raw onion.

Appetizers & Beverages

Deviled Eggs

4 hard-cooked eggs, cut in 1/2 lengthwise
1/2 tsp. salt
1/2 tsp. dry mustard
Dash of cayenne
1 tsp. herb vinegar
1 tsp. melted butter

Slip out egg yolks into a bowl. Mash with a fork and blend in remaining ingredients. Fill the whites with the egg-yolk mixture, place on a bed of chopped lettuce and refrigerate until ready to serve. For an extra-tasty touch, try adding 1 teaspoon of onion juice to the egg-yolk mixture. Serves 4.

Teas

It was considered sound practice to give each slave a "cleaning out' in the spring. Mistress would line up every man, woman, and child and administer to each a tablespoon of spring tonic, usually a mixture of molasses, sulphur and sassafras tea. Today's version, still taken in the spring by the older generation are the following teas.

Sassafras Tea (Spring Tonic)

4 large pieces of sassafras bark   6 tsp. (level) sugar
6 C. boiling water

Select the outer, rosy bark from the sassafras roots. Put the bark in a teapot. Pour boiling water over it. Cover and steep until tea is desired strength and color. Strain. Add sugar. Serves 6.

Beef Tea
(For Low Blood And Sickly, Spindly Types)

Cut desired amount of raw beef into tiny pieces. Put in a jar that will not break in boiling water. Add a broken knuckle of veal. Put a top on the jar. Put the jar in a pan of boiling water to cover and simmer for 8 hours. Drain off the juice in the jar and let it cool to a jelly. To make the tea, add 1 cup of hot water to a teaspoon of jelly.

Chamomile Tea
(For The Jitters Or When Feeling Indisposed)

1 C. boiling water   1 tsp. sugar
2 tsp. chamomile flowers

Pour boiling water over the flowers. Cover tightly and steep for 3 minutes. Strain into a hot cup and add sugar.

Ginger Tea (For Cold And Cramps)

2-1/2" long gingerroots or 1/2   1 C. boiling water
    tsp. ground ginger   Dash of salt

Crush the roots between towels or waxed paper. Put into teapot. Add boiling water. Cover and steep for 3 minutes. Strain and serve hot with sugar.

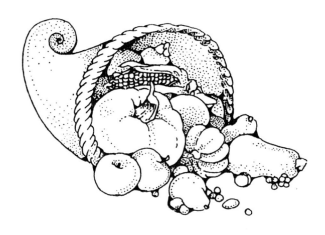

Punch

3 C. sugar
1 qt. water
1 large can unsweetened pineapple juice
4 bottles ginger ale or 7-Up
2 small cans lemon juice or 7 oz. bottle ReaLemon juice

Mix sugar and water together. Add pineapple juice and lemon juice. Add ginger ale or 7-Up last. May add 1 quart sherbet to mixture.

Orange Blossom Punch

3 C. orange juice
1-10 oz. can frozen strawberry or peach daiquiri mix concentrate, thawed
2 C. cold water
1-750 millimeter bottle champagne or sparkling white grape juice, chilled ice cubes

In a punch bowl, combine orange juice and thawed concentrate. Add 2 cups cold water. Stir to combine. Gently add champagne or grape juice, but do not stir. If desired, garnish with strawberries and orange wedges. Serve. Serves 12.

Hot Apple Toddy

4 C. apple juice
2 T. brown sugar, packed
12 whole cloves
1 tsp. ground nutmeg
2 large apples, peeled, cored and quartered

1 C. brandy
3/4 C. dark rum
3" stick cinnamon
Butter

In saucepan, mix apple juice, sugar and spices. Simmer, covered, for 20 minutes. Add apples. Simmer, covered, until tender, about 10 minutes. Strain. Return liquid to saucepan. Add liquors. Heat through. Place an apple quarter and dot of butter in each mug. Makes 7 (6 ounces) servings.

Wassail

1 large can pineapple juice
32 oz. cranberry juice
1 3/4 C. water
1 C. brown sugar

8 cinnamon sticks
1/2 orange peel or 1/2 orange
1 jigger of rum per glass, if desired

Put pineapple juice, water and cranberry juice in bottom of 8-cup percolator. Add rest of ingredients in top. Perk for 10 minutes. Serve in mugs or punch cups.

Dandelion Wine

5 lbs. dandelions (flowers only) 2 cakes of yeast
5 lbs. sugar

Boil flowers in water to cover. Add sugar and crumbled yeast cakes. Put into crock. Let stand for 15 days. Strain off dandelions. Add more sugar, if needed. Let stand for 15 more days. Taste for alcoholic content. If not strong enough, add more sugar. Bottle.

Grape Wine

Put Concord grapes in crock. Pour scalding hot water over grapes. Use 1 gallon of water to each 2 quarts of grapes. Cover the grapes and let them cool. Add one yeast cake and 2 pounds of sugar. Let the grapes set for 5 days. Strain off pulp and grapes. Discard. Add 2 pounds more sugar to wine and put it in large jars. Cover lightly. Let the wine set until it stops bubbling, about 1 week. Strain. Avoid as much of the sediment as possible. Add sugar to taste. Bottle and cap. Use same process for raisin wine.

Dandelion Wine

1 qt. dandelion blossoms 2 lbs. sugar
1 gal. boiling water 1 cake yeast
1 lemon and 2 oranges

Put flowers in a jar. Pour boiling water over them. Let stand 3 days. Grate lemon and oranges, the peel, juice and all. Simmer with juice and blossoms for 15 minutes. Pour over sugar and when lukewarm; add yeast. Set away, covered, for 8 to 10 days. Then strain and bottle.

Soup

Turtle Soup

Making the Turtle Soup was a social event for the men. When they decided to "snap" the turtle, the women would take out a bottle of homemade wine or cider, fill some glasses with ice, set them on the kitchen table, and excuse themselves. The next few hours were a mystery, but the end result was magnificent.

The Women's Version Of Turtle Soup

1 1/2 qts. chicken broth
1 lb. turtle meat, bone and gristle removed
3 T. chicken fat
1 onion, chopped
1 T. butter
Salt and pepper, to taste
1 T. chopped parsley
6 thin slices of lemon

Make a richly flavored chicken broth, seasoned with salt. Remove the chicken from the broth. Cut the turtle meat into small pieces. Brown it in the chicken fat. Sauté the onion in butter over medium heat until it is soft and yellow. Add turtle, onion, salt and pepper, and any fat left in pans to chicken broth. Bring to boil. Reduce heat and simmer for 10 minutes. Serve with parsley and lemon slice. Serves 4 to 6.

The Men's Version Of Turtle Soup
(Or As Close To It As They'll Care To Let Us Get)

3 lbs. turtle meat	6 cloves
3 1/2 qts. water	1 tsp. sugar
2 onions, chopped	1 C. canned tomatoes
1 stalk celery, chopped	1 T. salt
1/2 bay leaf	1/2 tsp. peppercorns
2 sprigs parsley	3 T. butter

Cut the meat and gristle from the bones. Add the meat, bones and gristle to the water. Add all remaining ingredients, except butter. Heat to boiling. Reduce heat and simmer, covered, for 1 hour. Remove vegetables, bones and gristle. Cut the turtle meat into small pieces and brown slowly in the butter. Add the meat and any drippings to the broth. Bring to a boil. Reduce heat and simmer for 25 minute. Add more salt and pepper, if needed. Serves 8 to 10.

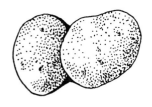

Shrimp Chowder

3-4 1/2 to 5 oz. cans shrimp
1/4 C. chopped onion
2 T. melted fat or oil
1 C. boiling water
1 C. diced potatoes

1/2 tsp. salt
Dash of pepper
2 C. milk
Chopped parsley

Drain shrimp and rinse with cold water. Cut large shrimp in half. Cook onion in fat until tender. Add boiling water, potatoes and seasonings. Cover and cook for 15 minutes or until potatoes are tender. Add milk and shrimp. Heat. Garnish with parsley. Serves 6.

Baked Potato Soup

4 large baked potatoes
2/3 C. butter
2/3 C. flour
6 C. milk

3/4 tsp. salt
1/2 tsp. pepper
1/2 C. cheese

Melt butter and add flour. Heat 1 minute. Add milk. Stir until thick. Add other ingredients. Mash potatoes and stir in. Serve with sour cream, cheese, bacon bits, parsley, etc.

Carrot Soufflé

1/2 C. butter or margarine
1 T. flour
1/4 tsp. salt
3 eggs
1 tsp. baking powder

1 tsp. vanilla
2 C. cooked carrots, mashed
1 C. sugar
1/2 tsp. nutmeg

In mixing bowl, blend flour and melted butter or margarine. Add remaining ingredients. Pour mixture into a casserole dish, sprayed lightly with Pam. Bake at 350° for 40 minutes.

Black Bean Soup

2 C. black beans	1 tsp. salt
1 onion, sliced	Dash of pepper
3 T. butter	Dash of cayenne
2 sprigs parsley	Juice and rind of 1 lemon
2 stalks celery, sliced	2 T. flour
1 carrot, sliced	1 hard-boiled egg

Soak the beans in water to cover for 12 hours. Drain. Sauté the onion in melted butter for about 5 minutes. add the beans, 2 quarts of water, parsley, celery, carrot, salt, pepper, cayenne and lemon juice and rind. Cover and simmer 3 1/2 to 4 hours, adding more water, if necessary. Press mixture through a sieve. Reheat over boiling water. Make the flour into a paste by mixing with 3 tablespoons of cold water. Add to soup. Cook and stir until thick and smooth. add more salt and pepper, if necessary. Chop the egg and add to soup. Serves 6 to 8.

Vegetable Beef Soup

2 C. cubed stew beef	1/2 C. chopped potatoes
1 to 2 lbs. beef marrow bones	1/2 C. elbow macaroni
1/2 C. dried lima beans	1/2 C. chopped onions
3 T. barley	1 white turnip, chopped
3 T. rice	1/4 C. chopped parsnip
3 T. kidney beans	2 C. canned stewed tomatoes
1/2 C. chopped celery	1 C. whole kernel corn
1/2 C. dried peas	Salt and pepper, to taste

Cover beef and bones with cold water in large soup pot. Cover and simmer until meat is tender. Add beans, peas, barley, rice and kidney beans with 8 cups of cold water. Bring to boiling point. Add next seven ingredients. Simmer slowly about 2 to 2 1/2 hours. Add water as it cooks away. Add corn and any other available raw or cooked vegetables 1/2 hour before end of cooking time. Remove bones. Add salt and pepper to taste. This soup will be quite thick. Serves 8.

Salads

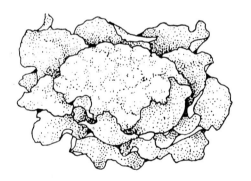

Macaroni Salad

1-8 oz. pkg. dry elbow macaroni
1 T. salt
3 qts. water
1/2 C. chopped celery
1/4 C. diced green pepper
2 T. (or more) thinly sliced radishes
3/4 C. mayonnaise or salad dressing
2 T. prepared mustard
1/4 tsp. onion salt

Cook macaroni in 3 quarts salted, boiling water for 11 minutes. Rinse with cold water. Drain. Combine all ingredients. Toss lightly. Chill for several hours.

Cranberry Salad

1 can cranberries
1 C. sour cream
1 small can crushed pineapple
Pinch of salt
1 env. unflavored gelatin
1/2 C. pineapple juice

Sprinkle gelatin over 1/2 cup juice. Let dissolve over hot water. Stir in cranberry mixture. Refrigerate.

Granny's Salad

Layer of shredded lettuce
Layer of shredded carrots
Layer of sliced radishes, if desired
Layer of canned peas, drained

Dot with mayonnaise. Put a little grated onion on each dot and then about 1/4 teaspoon sugar on top of onions. Continue with layers of vegetables until you have desired amount. Cover with shredded lettuce and crumbled, crisp fried bacon. Can be made several hours before serving.
NOTE: Use any combination of vegetables you desire.

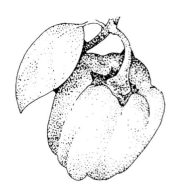

Cabbage-Apple Salad

2 C. shredded cabbage
2 C. diced apples
2 T. slivered almonds, toasted
1/3 C. salad dressing
1 T. lemon juice
1 tsp. sugar
1/2 tsp. salt

Combine ingredients and mix well. Serves 6.

Carrot-Apple Salad

1 large carrot, shredded
3 C. diced apples
1/3 C. raisins
1/3 C. salad dressing or mayonnaise

1 T. lemon juice, if desired
1/8 tsp. salt

Combine ingredients and mix well.

Cucumber Salad

3 large cucumbers
1 pod garlic, diced
Paprika, to taste
1/2 pt. sour cream

1 small onion, chopped
Black pepper, to taste
1 pinch of red pepper
2 T. cider vinegar

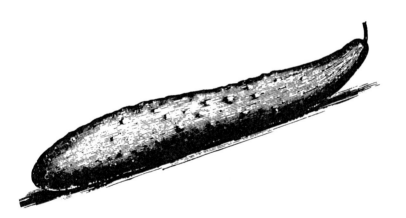

Slice each cucumber and salt heavy. Cover bowl and place in refrigerator for 24 hours. Squeeze all of the water out of cucumbers. Add rest of ingredients and mix well. Replace cover and put in refrigerator until needed to serve.

Potato Salad

10 lbs. potatoes, cooked, peeled and cubed
1 C. chopped onions
1 C. chopped celery
12 hard-boiled eggs, cut up
1 qt. mayonnaise
1/4 C. prepared mustard
Salt, pepper and paprika, to taste
1 C. sweet relish
1/4 C. sugar

Combine potatoes, onions, eggs and celery in large bowl. Combine mayonnaise, relish, mustard, sugar, salt, pepper and paprika. When thoroughly mixed, fold into potato mixture. Refrigerate and serve when well chilled. Serves 30.

Hog Maw Salad

4 lbs. hog maws
1 1/2 C. celery
1 green pepper
2 onions
2 C. mayonnaise
Salt and pepper

Cook hog maws in boiling water until tender. Remove fatty parts. Chop them finely and let them cool. Finely chop celery, green pepper and onions. Add to the hog maws and bind with 2 cups mayonnaise. Season with salt and pepper.

At first, I though I was eating chicken salad!

Breads

Drop Dumplings (Strip Dumplings)

1 C. sifted flour
1 1/2 tsp. baking powder
1/4 tsp. baking soda
1/4 tsp. salt
1/2 C. buttermilk

Sift the dry ingredients three times. Mix the dry ingredients and the buttermilk. Mix slightly with a fork. Put on a floured board, and knead a few times. Roll out 1/4" thick. Cut into strips with a knife. Drop into boiling soup or stew. Cover and let boil gently for 12 minutes. Do not uncover during cooking. Makes 10 to 12 Strip Dumplings.

Drop Dumplings

1 C. sifted flour
1 1/2 tsp. baking powder
3/4 tsp. salt
1 egg
1/3 C. milk

Sift flour, baking powder and salt into a bowl. Beat egg; add milk. Add egg-milk mixture to dry ingredients. Drop by teaspoonfuls into hot chicken broth. Cover and cook 10 to 12 minutes.
NOTE: Dumplings may be cooked in boiling, salted water (1 teaspoon salt to 1 quart of water).

Plain Pancakes

2 C. flour
1 1/2 T. baking powder
1 1/2 T. sugar
3/4 tsp. salt
1/4 tsp. cream of tartar

2 eggs
1 1/2 C. milk
3 T. melted shortening
1 tsp. vanilla

Sift the dry ingredients together into a bowl. Mix the eggs, milk and shortening. Add to dry ingredients. Stir until the flour is moistened. (The batter will be lumpy.) Fry on a hot skillet or griddle. Makes 6 good-sized pancakes.

This was the favorite breakfast that Grams, Fa-Fa and Grandma Charlotte (Sis. Weldon, P.G.W.M.) made for all of her grandchildren.

Rolls

1 1/4 C. milk
1 yeast cake
1/3 C. sugar
3/4 C. butter or margarine
1 tsp. salt
3 eggs
5 1/2 C. flour

Warm 1/4 cup of the milk and dissolve the yeast cake in it. Set aside. Dissolve remaining milk, sugar, butter or margarine and salt together over low heat. Beat eggs and add to liquid. Add yeast. Blend in flour. If dough is too soft to handle, add a little more flour. Grease on top. Cover thinly with melted butter and dust lightly with flour to handle. Cut into triangles, like pizza wedges. Roll triangles from wide end. Bake on two greased baking sheets in 325° oven until light brown, about 20 minutes. Serves 8 to 10.

My grandfather said he felt he had to eat a dozen before he felt he had any bread in his mouth. These rolls are feather-light an freezable.

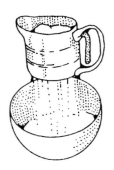

Deep-Fat Fried Puffs

Prepare a dough for rolls, but add 2/3 cup of sugar to the dry ingredients. Roll out dough and cut into desired shapes. Fry in deep fat and sprinkle with brown sugar.

Fried Bread

Any leftover dough   Deep-fat, for frying

Take the dough, "Slap it on the bottom, and stick it in the fat."

Fried Bread is something hot and sweet. It is a good way to use leftover dough.

Buttermilk Rolls

1 3/4 C. buttermilk
1/4 C. sugar
2 tsp. salt
3/4 C. oil
1/2 tsp. baking soda

1 pkg. dry yeast
3/4 C. lukewarm water
4 1/2 to 5 1/2 C. sifted flour
Melted butter

Scald buttermilk. Stir in sugar, salt, oil and baking soda. Cool to lukewarm. Dissolve yeast in warm water; add to buttermilk mixture. Stir in enough flour to make soft dough. Knead until smooth. Shape into rolls. Place in greased pans or on baking sheet. Brush tops with melted butter. Cover and let rise in warm place until double in size. Bake at 425° for 15 to 20 minutes.

Spoon Bread

1 1/2 C. milk
3/4 C. cornmeal
3/4 tsp. salt

3 eggs, separated
1 1/2 T. fat

Preheat oven to 375°. Scald the milk. Stir in the cornmeal and salt, and cook until thickened, stirring constantly. Add the lightly beaten egg yolks and the fat. Remove from heat and cool slightly. Fold in the stiffly beaten egg whites. Bake in well greased 8" baking dish for 35 to 40 minutes. Serves 4.

Whole Wheat Muffins

1 C. whole wheat flour
3/4 C. flour
1 T. baking powder
1 C. sugar
1 tsp. salt

3/4 C. milk
1/4 C. honey
3 T. oil
1 egg

Combine all dry ingredients. In separate bowl, mix together milk, honey, oil and egg. Stir into dry ingredients until they are just moistened. Spoon into greased and floured medium-sized muffin tin, filling each cup two-thirds full. Bake at 325° for 20 to 25 minutes.

Corn Bread

1 1/2 C. self-rising cornmeal
1/2 C. self-rising flour
1 tsp. sugar

1/4 C. shortening
3/4 C. milk
1 egg

Combine cornmeal, flour and sugar. Cut in shortening until mixture is crumbly. In separate bowl, combine milk and egg. Pour wet ingredients into dry ingredients and stir until well mixed. Pour into greased iron skillet or square baking pan. Bake at 425° for 25 minutes. Makes 6 to 8 servings.

Cheese Bread

1 pkg. active dry yeast
3/4 C. warm water (1 C. if egg mix is used)
2 1/2 to 3 C. flour
3 t. non-instant nonfat dry milk
1 T. sugar
1 tsp. salt
1 egg or 1/4 C. dry egg mix, packed
1 C. finely cut up or shredded cheese

Dissolve yeast in water. Mix 2 1/2 cups of the flour with rest of dry ingredients, including egg mix, if used. Add dissolved yeast, egg, if used, and cheese. Mix well. Add a little more flour, if needed to handle easily. Knead dough on lightly floured surface about 10 minutes. Place in a greased bowl. Turn dough so top will be greased. Cover lightly and let rise in warm place (85°) about 1 hour. Punch dough down in bowl. Cover and let rise about 30 minutes or until almost doubled. Shape into one round loaf. Place on greased baking pan. Cover with greased wax paper. Let rise 1 hour. Bake at 375° (moderate oven) for 30 to 35 minutes. Makes 1 loaf.

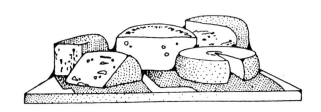

Cracklin Corn Bread

1/2 C. flour
1 C. yellow cornmeal
1 1/2 tsp. baking powder
1 tsp. salt
1/4 tsp. baking soda
2 tsp. sugar
1 C. buttermilk
1 egg, beaten
1/2 C. pork cracklings
1 T. bacon fat

Preheat oven to 450°. Heat 9" iron skillet in the oven 10 minutes. While skillet is heating, sift the flour, measure and sift three times, with the cornmeal, baking powder, salt, baking soda and sugar. Add buttermilk, egg and cracklings. Stir until well mixed. Remove skillet from oven. Coat inside of skillet with bacon fat. Pour batter into hot skillet. Bake for 20 minutes. Serve hot.

Hush Puppies

1 C. cornmeal	1/2 tsp. salt
1/4 C. flour	1/2 tsp. garlic salt
1/4 C. dry egg mix, packed	1 small onion, chopped
1/4 tsp. baking soda	1 C. buttermilk
1 tsp. baking powder	Fat or oil 1" deep in frypan

Stir dry ingredients together until well mixed. Add onion and milk. Mix well. Drop batter by teaspoonfuls into hot fat or oil. Fry 2 to 3 minutes or until browned on al sides. Drain well.

Cheese Biscuits

2 C. self-rising flour	1/2 C. Cheddar cheese
2 T. (heaping) shortening	3/4 C. milk

Mix flour and shortening with pastry cutter. Grate Cheddar cheese and add. Add milk. Flour a piece of wax paper well. Put dough on this and flour on top. Pat out biscuits with hands. Cut and place on foil-covered cookie sheet. May be covered with foil and frozen. When frozen, place in plastic bags and use as needed. Bake at 450° for 12 to 15 minutes.

Corn Bread Stuffing

1 1/2 large onions
1/2 stalk celery
2 large green peppers, seeded and sliced lengthwise
2 C. fresh mushrooms, sliced
1-10x20" pan of day-old corn bread, broken into crumbs
2 T. almond slivers
2 tsp. each pepper, thyme, sage and poultry seasoning
1/2 T. salt

Wash and finely dice the onions, celery, green peppers and mushrooms. Sauté the onions, celery, green peppers and mushrooms in butter until lightly browned. Remove from heat and add corn bread crumbs, almond slivers, pepper, thyme, sage, poultry seasoning and salt. This will stuff an 18 pound turkey.

Hoe Cakes (Flour Method)

2 C. flour
1 1/2 tsp. baking powder
1 tsp. salt
2 tsp. lard
About 2 C. boiling water

Mix the flour, baking powder, salt and lard in a bowl. Add enough of the boiling water, to make a batter stiff enough to hold a shape. Heat some shortening in a cast-iron skillet until it is sizzling hot. The fat should be at least 1/8" deep. Shape the dough into flat cakes, and fry on each side until they are a rich golden brown. Do not turn the cakes until they are the right color. Serve with jelly or butter.

Hot Water Corn Bread

2 C. plain cornmeal
1 1/2 T. flour
1 tsp. salt
Boiling water
Fat for deep frying

Mix the cornmeal, flour and salt together. Pour just enough of the boiling water over the mixture to moisten it. Form the mixture into pones—Oval shapes that are "quite a big bigger than a golf ball". And deep fry. This is very good with greens.

Vegetables

Pickled Beets

4 lbs. fresh beets
1 clove garlic, sliced
A few thick slices of onion
1 1/2 to 1 3/4 C. sugar,
    according to your preference
1 T. pickling spices
3/4 C. water
1 1/4 C. cider vinegar

Steam beets in small amount of water for 30 to 40 minutes or until crispy tender. Do not overcook. Drain. Rinse with cold water. Peel and slice. Place beets in four sterilized pint jars. Add garlic and onion slices. Combine sugar, pickling spices, water and vinegar in saucepan. Bring to boil. Pour over beets, filling jars to within 1" of tops. Seal tightly.

Green Tomato Chow-Chow

2 gals. green tomatoes, ground
6 green peppers, ground
6 onions, ground
2 T. cinnamon
5 C. vinegar
2 C. brown sugar
1 tsp. salt
2 T. cloves

Combine all ingredients in large kettle. Boil for 2 hours. Transfer ingredients to glass jars. Seal while hot.

Hoppin' Johns

1 C. raw rice	1 can black-eyed peas
2 C. water	1/2 lb. bacon
Dash of salt	1 medium onion, minced

Prepare rice to package directions. Bring 2 cups water to boil in medium saucepan; add dash of salt and hot sauce. Add 1 cup rinsed, washed rice. Stir, cover, turn to low heat and cook 20 minutes. While rice is cooking, cook bacon and onion until bacon is crisp. Drain and crumble bacon; reserve 1 tablespoon bacon fat. Add bacon-onion mixture, cooked rice and can of black-eyed peas. Stir and heat until hot.

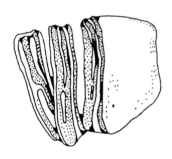

Mixed Greens

3 bunches turnip greens	2 ham hocks, preferable smoked
3 bunches mustard greens	Salt pork (optional)
6 to 8 T. bacon drippings	1 stick butter
2 T. sugar	Hot peppers to taste (optional)
Salt to taste	

Boil the ham hocks in water about 1 hour. Remove the stems from the greens and discard. Wash the leaves thoroughly, about 3 times. (This is time consuming.) Add greens to the ham hocks and salt pork if used. Add salt, sugar and bacon drippings. Simmer for about 2 hours. Add pared turnips the last hour. The last half hour add 1 stick of butter and the hot peppers.

Candied Yams

4 lbs. sweet potatoes
1 1/2 C. brown sugar
Juice of 1 lemon
1 stick margarine

Slice potatoes in saucepan. Add all other ingredients and cook over medium heat for 45 minutes or until the juice has become slightly thicker.

Cream Style Corn

1 dozen medium ears of sweet corn
3/4 T. salt
1 tsp. white pepper
1 1/2 T. bacon drippings

Cut corn off the cobs. Cook in heavy saucepan with other ingredients over low heat for 15 minutes. Stir often to make sure corn does not stick to pan. Stir in 1 cup of milk, thickened with 2 tablespoons of flour. Let simmer for a few minutes.

Five-Minute Cabbage

1 1/2 C. milk
4 C. (1 qt.) shredded cabbage
2 T. flour
2 tsp. margarine or butter
Salt and pepper, to taste

Heat milk and add cabbage. Boil gently for about 2 minutes. Mix the flour and margarine or butter and add a little hot milk from the cabbage. Stir this mixture into the cabbage. Cook and stir 3 or 4 minutes longer until thickened. Season with salt and pepper.

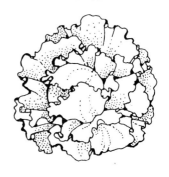

Fried Cabbage

1 head cabbage
Bacon or meat drippings
Salt and pepper, to taste

Shred a head of cabbage. Cover and fry slowly in bacon or meat drippings. Stir occasionally. Season with salt and pepper. Serve with corn bread.

Creamy Grits

1 C. regular cooking grits
5 C. boiling water
1 tsp. salt
1-3 oz. pkg. cream cheese
1/2 stick butter or margarine
1/2 pt. sour cream

Slowly stir grits into boiling, salted water and cook for 15 minutes, stirring occasionally. Add cream cheese, margarine and sour cream and stir until dissolved. Serves 6 to 8.

Fried Tomatoes

GREEN TOMATOES: Cut tomatoes into 1/2" slices. Dip in flour, seasoned with salt and pepper. Fry slowly in a small amount of hot fat until browned on both sides.
RIPE TOMATOES: Cut into 1/2" slices; dip in mixture of beaten egg and water and then into bread crumbs. Fry quickly in hot fat until brown on both sides. Season with salt and pepper.

Fried Green Tomatoes

1/2 C. flour
1/4 tsp. pepper
1/4 C. butter or margarine
1/2 tsp. salt
2 large green tomatoes, cut into 1/2" thick slices
2 T. plus 2 tsp. brown sugar, divided

Combine flour, salt and pepper. Dredge tomato slices in flour mixture. Melt butter in large skillet. Fry tomato slices on one side until browned. Remove from skillet and place in 9x13x2" baking dish, browned-side down. Top each tomato slice with 1 teaspoon brown sugar. Broil 3" from heat for 5 minutes or until brown and bubbly. Makes 4 servings.

Green Beans Superb

2 T. chopped onion
1 T. chopped green pepper
3 T. fat
1 tsp. salt
3 T. flour
Pepper
1 C. milk

1/2 C. bean stock
1 pimiento, chopped
1/4 C. grated cheese
2 C. cooked green beans, drained
1/2 tsp. paprika

Lightly brown onion and green pepper in fat; add flour, seasonings, milk and bean stock. Cook until thickened, stirring constantly. Remove from heat; add pimiento and cheese. Stir until cheese melts; pour over hot beans. Sprinkle with paprika. Serves 6.

Spinach

1 or 2 T. fat or oil
1/2 C. chopped onion
1 T. flour

1/2 C. water
1-10 oz. pkg. frozen spinach
Salt and pepper, to taste

Heat fat or oil in large frypan. Add onion and cook until tender. Add flour. Cook and stir until mixture begins to thicken. Add water and mix until smooth. Add spinach. Cover and cook about 15 minutes, stirring occasionally as spinach thaws. Season with salt and pepper.

"Low Country" Red Rice

1-6 oz. can tomato paste
4-6 oz. cans water
1 stick margarine

2 C. uncooked rice
Onions
Bell pepper

Melt margarine. Add onions and bell pepper. Add tomato paste and water. Bring to boil. Add rice. Boil hard a couple of minutes. Lower fire and cook until done, stirring occasionally.

Okra Gumbo

4 slices bacon
1 green pepper, chopped
2-10 oz. boxes frozen okra, thawed and drained
2 T. Worcestershire sauce
1 medium onion, sliced thin
2 ribs celery, sliced
1-16 oz. can chopped tomatoes, undrained
1/2 tsp. sugar
1/4 tsp. salt

Fry bacon until crisp; drain and set aside. Pour off half of drippings. Sauté onions in drippings until golden. Stir in green pepper and celery. Sauté until crisp, but tender. Add remaining ingredients, except bacon. Cook over low heat for about 60 minutes, stirring every 15 minutes. Serve over rice. Crumble bacon on top.

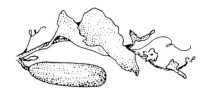

Scalloped Cucumbers

4 medium cucumbers, peeled and diced
1 1/2 C. milk
1 tsp. salt
1/2 tsp. pepper
1 C. dry bread crumbs
4 T. butter

Combine cucumbers, milk, salt and pepper thoroughly; fold in bread crumbs. Pour into greased 1-quart casserole; dot with butter. Bake at 350° for 30 minutes. Serves 4 to 6.

Sauerkraut Slaw

1-14 oz. can sauerkraut, drained
1/2 can water chestnuts, sliced and drained
1 C. diced celery
1/3 C. oil
1 C. green peppers
1/2 can garbanzo beans, drained

3/4 C. sugar
1/3 C. shredded cabbage
1/2 C. onion
1/4 C. pimientos
1 tsp. salt
Dash of pepper

Mix ingredients and chill together.

Spanish Rice

1/2 C. uncooked rice
1 T. fat or oil
1 small onion
1/2 green pepper, optional

1 stalk celery, optional
2 1/2 C. cooked or canned tomatoes
2 1/2 C. cut up, canned chopped meat or canned luncheon meat

Cook rice in fat or oil until lightly browned. Chop onion, green pepper and celery, if used. Add to rice. Stir in tomatoes. Heat to boiling. Lower heat. Cover and cook about 25 minutes or until rice is tender. Add meat to rice and heat until meat is hot. Serves 6.

Boiled Navy Beans

1 lb. dried navy beans
6 C. cold water
1/4 lb. salt pork
1 onion
1 pod red pepper
2 tsp. sugar
1 tsp. salt

Wash beans in cold water. Drain. Put beans in a 3- or 4-quart saucepan. Add remaining ingredients. Cover and bring to a boil. Lower heat and simmer for 2 1/2 to 3 hours. Stir occasionally to prevent sticking. Serves 4 to 6.
VARIATION: Black-eyed peas can be substituted for navy beans.

Main Dishes & Meat Dishes

Pig's Feet

6 medium-sized pig's feet
1 C. apple cider vinegar
1 large onion, chopped
1 green pepper, sliced
1 clove garlic, minced
2 bay leaves
1/8 tsp. cayenne pepper or 1 hot pepper
Salt, to taste
Pepper, to taste

Wash and clean pig's feet. Simmer in water and vinegar for 2 hours. Add onion, green pepper, garlic, bay leaves, cayenne pepper, salt and pepper. Simmer for another 2 hours or until meat is fork-tender. Drain feet from liquid and serve with vegetables.

Oxtails

4 oxtails, cut into 2 pieces
1 C. flour
Salt, to taste
Pepper, to taste
1 clove garlic, minced
Oil
1 onion, chopped

Combine flour, salt and pepper. Trim fat from oxtails. Wash. Pat dry. Dredge in seasoned flour. Sprinkle with garlic. Brown tails on all sides in hot oil. Drain off fat. Add onion to tails and cover with water. Cook slowly until tender, about 2 hours. Serve with rice, buttered lima beans and salad.

Fried Chicken

We're spoiled when it comes to chicken. It not only has to taste right, but smell and look right. The crust has to be a crunchy reddish-golden brown.

Cut the chicken into desired pieces, and fold wing tips under the main part of wings. Rinse in cold water and dry thoroughly. Dry chicken is less likely to burn. Flour the chicken in a paper bag with salt, pepper, paprika and poultry seasoning added to the flour. Heat a mixture of shortening (lard or vegetable shortening) and bacon fat in a cast-iron skillet (the mixture of lard and bacon fat gives the chicken the best taste and color). Fat should cover half of the chicken. When the fat is sizzling hot, put the chicken in a pan, but do not crowd the pieces. They should not touch each other. Cover the skillet and cook over high heat for 5 minutes. Remove cover, lower heat to medium and continue cooking until the chicken is brown on one side. Turn the pieces over, cover and cook over high heat for 5 minutes. Remove cover, lower heat, and cook over low light heat until the chicken is tender, about 20 minutes. Drain on paper towels.
NOTE: A cast-iron skillet is the best frypan. It should be pitted and rough and dark black in color. These are hard to come by now. Cakes and casseroles can also be baked in iron skillets.

Turtle

TO KILL AND SHELL A TURTLE: The first thing to do is cut off the head. Make the turtle grasp at stick. It will grasp the stick firmly in its jaws. The head then can be pulled forward and chopped off. The body must then be removed from the shell. Run a sharp knife around the edges of the skin where it joins the shell. Pull back the skin on the legs to the feet. Remove the lower part of the shell by cutting through the bridges, which join the two shells. Cut close to the lower part of the shell. With snappers and soft shelled turtles, this can be done with a sharp knife. With terrapins, this must be done with a hatchet or a saw. Having cut the bridges, the under shell can be removed by inserting a knife under it and lifting it off. Then entrails may be removed and the four quarters taken out of the upper shell. Cover the turtle meat with cold water and salt. Cover container and put in refrigerator overnight. Drain off water and rinse thoroughly in clear water.

Turtle meat is usually used for soup. A large pot of it was always kept on the back of the stove and was constantly enriched with vegetables and leftovers.

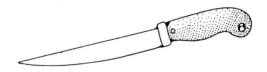

Sweet "N" Smoky Ribs

4 lbs. baby back ribs
2 T. liquid hickory smoke
1/2 tsp. black pepper
1/2 tsp. salt
1 clove garlic, minced
2 T. olive oil
1/2 C. ketchup
2 T. cider vinegar
1 T. sugar
1/2 C. orange juice

Parboil slices of ribs. Cook 20 minutes in a steamer rack over pan of water. Cool; remove any visible fat. Place in flat glass pan. Combine liquid smoke, pepper, salt, garlic, oil, ketchup, vinegar, sugar and orange juice and pour over the ribs. Cover tightly and refrigerate for 2 to 8 hours. Coat the grill with cooking oil. Preheat 5 minutes. Discard marinade and place ribs on grill in single layers.

Barbecue Sauce

1 medium onion
2 T. butter
2 T. brown sugar
4 T. lemon juice
2 bottles catsup
3 T. Worcestershire sauce
1/2 T. mustard
1 C. water
Salt and pepper, to taste

Brown butter in frypan. Add other ingredients and simmer. Pour mixture over meat. In a jar or blender, mix 2 tablespoons flour with water and thicken sauce like gravy. Leftover barbecue sauce is good over chicken or pork chops. It may be frozen in ice trays, flipped out and put in bags to be used as wanted.

Beef Brisket

3 1/2 to 4 lb. brisket	1 1/2 T. salt
1/4 tsp. pepper	1 tsp. dry mustard
1/2 C. water	1 T. Worcestershire sauce
1/4 C. vinegar	1/2 C. brown sugar
Lawry's seasoning salt	1 medium onion, sliced
3 T. catsup	Garlic powder

Combine salt, pepper and mustard. Rub both sides of meat. Sear on top of stove. Mix water, vinegar, brown sugar and Worcestershire sauce. Put meat in cooking bag and put in onion slices (may add carrot). Add slight pinch of oregano and rosemary. Bake at 325° for 3 to 3 1/2 hours. Store in refrigerator. Skim off fat slice on angle. Arrange in roasting pan and pour Bar-B-Que sauce over. Cover with foil and heat in 350° oven for 3/4 hour.
NOTE: Best prepared 2 days ahead of time; flavor improves with reheating.

Fancy Fast Chicken

3 whole chicken breasts	2 C. herb stuffing mix
6 slices Swiss cheese	1 stick margarine, melted
1 can cream of chicken soup	1/4 lb. fresh mushrooms
1/2 C. dry white wine	

Preheat oven to 350°. Place chicken in lightly greased 9x13" pan. Top each piece with cheese. Arrange sliced mushrooms over the cheese. Mix soup and wine; pour over the chicken. Sprinkle stuffing mix over the top and drizzle on melted butter. Bake 50 to 60 minutes or until chicken is cooked through. Makes 6 servings.
NOTE: Can use boneless breasts; cook 45 to 50 minutes.

Ham Hocks And Black-Eyed Peas

3 C. dry black-eyed peas
1/2 C. water
3 lbs. smoked ham hocks
1 1/4 C. chopped onions
1 C. chopped celery

1 tsp. salt
1/8 tsp. cayenne
1 bay leaf
1-10 oz. pkg. frozen cut okra

Rinse peas. In 6-quart Dutch oven, combine water and peas. Bring to boiling; simmer 2 minute. Remove from heat; cover and let stand 1 hour or combine water and peas and soak overnight. Do not drain. Stir in hocks, onions, celery, salt, cayenne and bay leaf. Bring to boiling. Cover and simmer until hocks are tender and beans are done, about 1 1/2 hours. Stir in okra; cook until very tender, 10 to 15 minutes. Discard bay leaf. Season to taste. Serves 6.

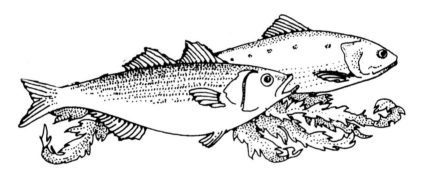

Pan-Fried Fish

2 lbs. fresh
　or steaks or 4-8 oz. pan-
　dressed fish
1 egg, beaten

2 T. water
1/4 C. finely crushed saltine
　crackers or cornmeal
Shortening

Thaw frozen fish. Cut fillets or steaks into six portions. Combine egg and water. Mix cracker crumbs or cornmeal, 1/2 teaspoon salt and dash of pepper. Dip fish into egg mixture; then roll in crumbs. Heat small amount of shortening in skillet; add fish in single layer. Fry over medium heat until browned on one side, 4 to 5 minutes. Turn; brown other side until fish flakes easily when tested with a fork, 4 to 5 minutes more. Drain on paper toweling. Makes 6 servings for fillets and steaks; 4 servings for pan-dressed fish.

Plantation Spareribs

1/2 C. sorghum
1/4 C. prepared mustard
1/4 C. vinegar
2 T. Worcestershire sauce
1/2 tsp. salt
1/2 tsp. bottled hot pepper sauce
4 lbs. pork spareribs

In small saucepan, blend sorghum into mustard; stir in the vinegar, Worcestershire sauce, salt and hot pepper sauce. Bring to boiling. Place spareribs, meaty-side down, in shallow roasting pan. Roast for 450° for 30 minutes. Remove pan from oven; drain off excess fat. Turn ribs, meaty-side up. Reduce oven temperature to 350°; roast until tender, about 1 hour more. During the last 30 minutes of roasting, baste frequently with sorghum mixture. Garnish with parsley sprigs and candied kumquats, if desired. Makes 6 to 8 servings.

Wild Duck

Start oven at 350°. Season duck with salt and pepper, cavity and all over. Pour melted butter over them. Brown both sides in oven. Melt butter on burner. Mix red wine. Pour over duck and then keep basting. Turn oven down to 325°. Cook for 2 hours, basting constantly.
SAUCE: Mix 1/2 cup broth from duck, 1 cup orange or grapefruit juice and 3/4 cup brandy; pour over just before serving.

Quail

Flour quail as for fried chicken. When nice and brown, place in roaster. Cover with foil. Bake at 350° for 15 to 20 minutes. Turn oven down very low. Bake for 1 hour. Melt 1 cup butter and 1 cup sherry; baste quail constantly. Enough for about 12 quail.

Pheasant

Brown pheasant, then place in roaster with a couple of bay leaves. Slice one onion over each bird. Pour 1 tablespoon bourbon. Then melt butter; dribble some over each bird. Barely cover bottom of roaster with water or wine. Baste with plain butter. Steam at least 2 hours at 325°.

Carolina Meatballs

5 lbs. ground beef	Salt and pepper
1 1/2 lbs. pork sausage	1 tsp. oregano
2 C. bread crumbs	1 tsp. Worcestershire sauce
Whole bottle of parsley flakes	4 eggs
Minces onions, to taste	

Mix ingredients. Roll in small balls. Cover cookie sheet with foil and broil. May be frozen individually on foil-covered cookie sheet and then put in plastic bag or container. Use three jars spaghetti sauce when ready to serve.

Chicken Breasts In Sour Cream

1 C. sour cream
1 can cream of mushroom soup
6 strips bacon, cut in 1/2
6 medium-size boneless chicken breasts, cut in 1/2
Salt and pepper, to taste
2 pkgs. dried chipped beef

Season chicken lightly with salt and pepper. (Dried beef and bacon will provide additional seasoning.) Wrap each piece with strip of bacon. Secure with toothpicks, if necessary. Blend soup and sour cream. Line up chicken in large, shallow, lightly buttered baking dish or pan, putting three or four slices of beef under each piece of chicken. Pour soup-sour cream mixture over and bake, uncovered, in 300° oven for 2 to 2 1/2 hours. Serves 12.

Chitterlings

PAN-FRIED CHITTERLINGS: Dip boiled Chitterlings in cornmeal. Fry in hot shortening until brown.
DEEP-FAT FRIED CHITTERLINGS: Dip boiled Chitterlings in egg and then in crushed saltine crackers. Fry in deep hot fat (375°) until brown.

Grilled Catfish

4 (or more) Mississippi (or farm raised) catfish fillets, washed and cleaned

Sprinkle catfish fillets with garlic salt and pepper. Place them in a well oiled grill basket or on a well oiled grill rack. Grill, uncovered, directly over medium to hot coals, about 5 minutes per side or until fish flakes easily. Serves 4 or more.

Roast Duck Or Goose

A 5 or 6 pound duck is best for roasting. Wash the duck inside and out with cold water. Drain and wipe dry. Sprinkle the inside with salt. Cornbread stuffing is especially good with duck, but any desired stuffing may be used. If no stuffing is used, insert 1 cup each of thinly sliced apple and onion into the body cavity. This will absorb any of the gamey flavor. Discard the apples and onion after cooking the duck. The duck may or may not be trussed. Brush the outside with the salad oil and sprinkle with salt and pepper. Place duck, breast-side up, on a rack in an open roasting pan. Roast in a 350° oven for 40 to 45 minutes per pound. Baste frequently with drippings. Use the brown drippings and some of the fat to make a gravy for the stuffing, if a stuffing was used.

Omit any fat in stuffing for a goose, because the fat under the skin drains into the stuffing. A goose must be trussed. Pour off some of the fat during cooking.

Strata 9x13" Dish

16 slices bread	6 eggs
Chopped ham	3 C. milk
1 can mushrooms, drained	1/2 tsp. mustard
8 slices Cheddar or Swiss cheese	Salt and pepper

Remove crust from 16 slices of bread. Grease pan. Layer eight slices of bread on bottom. Layer chopped ham, one can drained mushrooms, eight slices Cheddar or Swiss cheese. Add another layer of bread. Mix together eggs, milk, mustard, salt and pepper; pour over bread. Cover with foil and refrigerate overnight. Bake at 350° for 1 hour. Leave foil on for 20 minutes before serving.

Roast Goose (For Christmas Dinner)

1-10 lb. young goose
2 tsp. salt
1/2 recipe apricot stuffing
1 recipe wild rice and chestnut stuffing

1 orange, juice and rind
3 T. lemon juice

Wipe goose dry, but do not stuff. Place in open roasting pan. Prick through the skin into the fat layer around the legs and wings. Heat in a moderately hot (375°) oven for 15 minutes. Remove and let cool to room temperature; repeat this procedure two more times, draining the grease from the pan each time. Rub goose with salt. Fill with fruit stuffing in neck cavity and the rice stuffing in larger cavity. Truss; weigh to estimate cooking time, if possible. Place breast up on rack in an uncovered roasting pan in a moderately slow (325°) oven, allowing 25 minutes for each pound. (If the goose weighs 8 pounds or less, roast in a moderately hot (375°) over, allowing 35 minutes per pound. Basting is unnecessary, but if desired and grated rind of one orange and the lemon may be sprinkled over the breast during baking period. A frozen goose does very well and a 10 pound goose will feed 10 people, but don't expect to have any leftovers.
NOTE: You can save the goose grease to be used for winter colds.

Wild Rice And Chestnut Stuffing

1 C. wild rice
1/2 C. melted butter or other fat
1/8 tsp. pepper
1/2 lb. chestnuts, blanched and cooked
1/4 tsp. salt
2 T. minced onion

Wash rice thoroughly and steam, using 3 cups of water and 1 teaspoon salt, for about 40 minutes or until tender. Drain. Add remaining ingredients and toss lightly. Fills a 4 pound fowl.

TO SHELL AND BLANCH CHESTNUTS: Place the chestnuts in cold water; discard those which float. Dry and split each shell 1/2 to 3/4" on each side. Place in saucepan and add 1 1/2 tablespoons cooking oil and shake pan over heat for 5 minutes. After cooling, remove shells and brown skin with sharp paring knife.

Smothered Chicken

Cut up chicken, place in pan and sprinkle with salt, pepper and 3 tablespoons of finely chopped green pepper. Put some strips of bacon over the top and bake in hot (350°) oven. Bake 1 hour. Remove the chicken and make a sauce of 3 tablespoons of fat from pan, 4 tablespoons flour and 1/2 cup of cream. Heat slowly and stir in nicely. Pour sauce over chicken and serve.

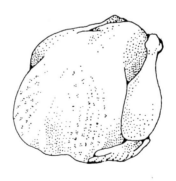

Ham Hocks

Put hocks in a large saucepan. Allow 1 per person. Add just enough hot salted water to cover. Cover the pan and bring to a boil. Reduce heat and simmer 2 1/2 to 3 hours or until hocks are tender. Place hocks in a baking dish in a hot (450°) oven to brown and dry out excess fat. Serve with greens.

Hog Chitlins and Maw

2 lbs. pork maw (hogs throat or mouth)
2 tsp. crushed red pepper flakes
4 small onions, finely chopped
5 lbs. precooked chitlins (hogs small intestine)
2 T. salt
4 ribs celery, finely chopped
4 small green peppers, finely chopped, cooked and seeded

Wash pork maw several times in cold water. Drain well. Place in large pot. Fill cooking pot with cold water 2" above the meat. Add 2 tablespoons salt, red pepper flakes and half the celery, onions and green peppers. Heat to boiling. Reduce heat to simmering. Cover and cook until tender for 1 1/2 to 3 hours. Remove maw to platter to cool. Reserve cooking broth. Wash the chitlins several times in cold water. drain well. Place chitlins in large pot. Add enough of maw cooking liquid to cover by 2". Add remaining celery, onions and green peppers. Heat to boiling. Reduce heat to simmering. Cover and cook until tender, about 1 1/2 hours. When maw is cool enough to handle, cut into 1" pieces. when chitlins are tender, stir in maw pieces. Simmer together for 15 minutes. Season with salt and pepper.

Muskrat, Squirrel Or Rabbit

After the animals have been skinned and cleaned, disjoint it and soak in salted water or vinegar water for 2 hours. Make a thin batter of milk, eggs, flour, baking powder and salt. Dip meat pieces in batter and fry.

Smothered Pheasant

1 pheasant
Flour
Salt and pepper, to taste
1/2 C. consommé
1/2 C. dry red wine

5 stalks celery, cut into 3" lengths
5 or 6 medium onions, sliced
Butter
Thyme

Cut pheasant into pieces; dredge in a mixture of flour, salt and pepper. Place in roaster or Dutch oven; pour wine and consommé over pheasant. Place a piece of butter on each piece of pheasant; sprinkle with thyme and marjoram. Then cover with onions, celery stalks and celery leaves. Cover and bake at 450° for 30 minutes. Reduce heat and continue baking for 1 1/2 hours (2 hours, if needed). Baste during baking time. Remove lid and brown on 450° for 30 minutes before serving. Make gravy from pan juices. Yield: 4 servings.

Sweet And Sour Chicken

1/4 C. brown sugar
2 T. cornstarch
1/2 tsp. salt
3/4 C. liquid, drained from canned pineapple
1/4 C. vinegar
1 T. soy sauce
3 C. cooked chicken, cut in pieces

1/4 C. onion, thin half slices
1 C. pineapple chunks, canned and drained
1/2 C. celery strips, cut very thin, 1" long
1/2 C. green pepper rings, thin, quartered
2 T. pimiento, diced
1-3 oz. can chow mein noodles
1/4 C. almonds, slivered, toasted

Combine brown sugar, cornstarch and salt. Stir into pineapple liquid. Add vinegar and soy sauce. bring to a boil over high heat. Reduce heat and cook until thick, stirring constantly. Remove from heat. Add chicken, onion, pineapple, celery and green pepper. Cook 5 minutes. Add pimiento and cook 1 minute longer. Serve over chow mein noodles. Top with almonds. Serves 6.

Stuffed Green Peppers

5 to 6 green peppers
1/2 lb. lean ground beef
1/4 C. finely chopped onion
1 T. chopped pimiento
1 tsp. salt
1/2 C. cooked rice
1 T. Worcestershire sauce
1 tsp. prepared mustard
1-16 oz. can tomatoes
1/4 C. catsup, optional

Cut a slice off top of each pepper. Remove core, seeds and white membrane. In a small bowl, combine beef, onion, pimiento, salt and rice and catsup, if desired. Spoon into peppers. Stand peppers up in slow-cooking pot. Add Worcestershire sauce and mustard to tomatoes. Cover pot; cook on low, 8 to 10 hours. Serves 5 to 6.

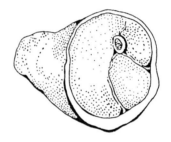

Party Chili (Recipe For A Crowd)

8 lbs. ground beef
2-15 oz. cans tomato sauce
8-24 oz. cans tomatoes
8-16 oz. cans kidney beans, drained and reserve liquid
8 C. chopped onions
1/4 C. sugar
6 T. chili powder
3 T. salt
4 T. flour, in water

Cook and stir ground beef and onion in large, heavy roaster until meat is brown and onion is tender. Stir in tomatoes, liquid from kidney beans and tomato sauce. Mix chili powder, flour and salt together and add to mixture. Add beans and simmer, uncovered, for 1 hour and 15 minutes or until desired consistency.

Lasagna (Recipe For A Crowd)

2 pkgs. lasagna noodles
5 lbs. hamburger
1 large can diced tomatoes
2 cans mushroom soup
1 tsp. curry powder
Salt, pepper and garlic salt
2 pkgs. Swiss cheese

2 pkgs. mozzarella cheese
2 large containers cottage cheese
2 onions, diced
Parmesan cheese
Bread crumbs

Cook noodles according to directions. Sauté hamburger. Season with salt, pepper, garlic salt and onion. Pour off juice of tomatoes, dice, add 1 teaspoon sugar and add to meat mixture. Mix cottage cheese, mushroom soup and curry powder together. Line bottom of large pan with noodles. Put Swiss cheese diagonal. Add layer of hamburger mixture. Sprinkle mozzarella cheese. Add layer of cottage cheeses until mixture is used up. Top with bread crumbs and Parmesan cheese. Bake at 350° until bubbly along the side.
NOTE: I used bag shredded cheese.

Homemade Pork Sausage

2 lbs. fresh, lean ground pork loin or pork shoulder
2 dry, hot red pepper pods, finely chopped

1 T. salt
1 tsp. black pepper
2 tsp. sage

Put the meat and red pepper through a food chopper. Add the salt, pepper and sage. Shape meat into patties. Brown on both sides in an iron skillet. Reduce. Heat, cover and cook slowly until done, about 20 minutes. Meat is grayish white in the center when done.

Leontyne Price Shrimp Gumbo

1/2 C. chopped onion
5 T. butter
3 T. flour
4 1/2 C. chicken broth or bouillon
1-1 lb. can tomatoes
1 tsp. salt
2 tsp. minced parsley
1/4 tsp. thyme
1 clove garlic, minced
2 bay leaves
2 C. cooked okra (I use the frozen okra in packages)
1 tsp. gumbo file
1 1/2 lbs. shrimp (raw or packaged)
1-6 oz. can frozen or can crab meat
3 C. hot cooked rice

Sauté onion in 2 tablespoon butter for 5 minutes. Add remaining butter; melt and blend in flour. Add broth, stirring until smooth. Add next six ingredients. Simmer, covered for 1 hour. Add okra, gumbo file, shrimp and crab meat. Simmer 10 minutes. Remove bay leaves. Serve over rice. Yield: 5 servings.

Hog Maw, Pig Feet, Pig Tails and Pig Ears

Rinse meat in cold water. Boil in salted water to cover with onion and celery added, until tender. Hog maws take about 4 hours to cook. Pig feet takes about 6 hours. Pig tails take about 1 1/2 to 2 hours. Pig ears takes about 2 to 3 hours. Serve with vinegar and greens.

Neck Bones And Sauerkraut

5 lbs. neck bones
1 onion, chopped
2 large cans sauerkraut (1 qt.)
Salt and pepper, to taste

Cover neck bones with water. Add the onion. Let simmer until the water is almost gone and the meat is tender. Drain the sauerkraut and rinse in a colander. Place sauerkraut on top of neck bones. Add salt and pepper to taste. Simmer until the water has gotten almost to the bottom of the pan, about 35 minutes. Serves 6.

Cracklins

Fresh pork skins or 1 C. salt pork
   or slab bacon
Salt

Cut pork skin into small pieces. Cook in heavy pot or skillet until skin is crispy. Stir frequently so the skin doesn't burn. Drain drippings. Sprinkle cracklins with salt and let cool.

Brains And Eggs

1 lb. brains
Bacon fat
Salt, to taste
4 eggs, slightly beaten
Pepper, to taste

Pour boiling water over brains in colander to remove all membrane. Rinse under clear water. Pour some bacon fat in a skillet and sprinkle salt over bottom to keep brains from sticking. Heat fat over medium heat. Add brains and cook slowly 8 to 10 minutes. When brains are nearly done, add eggs. Sprinkle with pepper to taste and cook, stirring gently, until eggs are done. Serve with ketchup. Serves 4.
NOTE: A cast-iron skillet is the best frypan. It should be pitted and rough and dark black in color. These are hard to come by now. Cakes and casseroles can also be baked in iron skillets.

Tasty Ham 'N' Asparagus Bake

1 can chopped ham
1-10 1/2 oz. can cream of
   mushroom soup
1/2 C. milk
1-1 lb. 3 oz. can white asparagus spears
1 can French fried onion rings

Slice chopped ham into four equal parts. Blend together the mushroom soup and milk. Place the chopped ham slices in 2-quart casserole. Arrange the asparagus spears on top of the meat. Pour the soup over the asparagus. Sprinkle the onions over the top of the casserole. Cover and bake in 375° oven for about 20 minutes. Serve hot. Serves 4.

Ham Balls (Recipe For A Crowd)

2 1/2 lbs. ground ham
2 lbs. ground pork
1 lb. ground beef
3 eggs
3 C. crushed graham crackers

2 tsp. dry mustard
2 C. milk
2 cans tomato soup
3/4 C. vinegar
2 1/4 C. brown sugar

Mix meats together. Add eggs, crumbs and milk. Shape into 25 individual loaves or use 1/3 cup measure to make 36 large balls. Place in a shallow pan. Make a sauce, using the tomato soup, vinegar, brown sugar and dry mustard. Pour over balls and bake at 350° for 1 hour, basting as needed.

Crab-Rice Casserole

2-6 oz. pkgs. frozen crab meat
3 C. hot cooked rice
2 C. shredded Cheddar cheese
1-3 oz. pkg. cream cheese, room temp.

1 C. (1/2 pt.) sour cream
1/2 C. chopped onion
1/2 tsp. garlic salt
1/2 tsp. basil
1 medium tomato

Thaw crab meat. Combine crab meat, rice and 1 1/2 cups Cheddar cheese. Spoon half of mixture into shallow 1 1/2-quart baking dish. Beat cream cheese until smooth. Stir in sour cream, onion, garlic salt and basil; spoon half over crab meat mixture. Repeat, making second layers of each. Cover baking dish with foil, crimping it to edges. Bake in moderate (350°) oven for 30 minutes. Uncover. Sprinkle with remaining 1/2 cup Cheddar cheese. Cut tomato in three slices and then cut in half. Arrange half tomato slice on top of cheese. Return to oven for 5 to 10 minutes or until cheese is softened and tomato is hot. Serves 6.

Chicken Casserole

1 C. diced, cooked chicken
1 can water chestnuts
1 C. cooked celery
1 C. cooked rice
1 can cream of chicken soup
2 T. chopped onion
3/4 C. mayonnaise
1/2 C. almonds
TOPPING:
1 C. corn flakes
1/2 C. melted butter

Mix first eight ingredients together well. Mix corn flakes and melted butter on top of casserole. Bake at 350° for 45 minutes.

Cheese And Macaroni Delight

1-8 oz. pkg. elbow macaroni, cooked
1/4 C. butter, melted
1 tsp. chopped onion
1/4 C. flour
1 tsp. salt
1/8 tsp. pepper
2 C. milk
2 T. chopped parsley
1 tsp. dried sweet basil
1 pimiento, chopped
2 C. shredded sharp Cheddar cheese
6 eggs

Sauté onion in butter in saucepan. Add flour, salt and pepper; mix well. Stir in milk gradually. Cook, stirring constantly, until sauce is smooth and thickened. Add parsley, basil and pimiento. Stir in cheese, reserving 1/2 cup. Heat until cheese is melted. Combine with macaroni. Turn into 9" square, buttered baking dish. Make six depressions in top of macaroni mixture; break an egg into each one. Sprinkle reserved cheese on top, leaving eggs, uncovered. Bake at 350° for 30 minutes or until eggs are the desired firmness. Serves 6.

Grits And Sausage Casserole

1 C. uncooked quick-cooking grits (not instant)
1 lb. mild bulk pork sausage
8 eggs, beaten
1 1/2 C. milk
1/4 tsp. garlic salt
1/4 tsp. white pepper
3 T. lightly salted butter or margarine
2 C. (8 oz.) shredded sharp Cheddar cheese

Cook grits according to package directions. Set aside. Cook sausage over medium heat until browned, stirring to crumble. Drain well and set aside. If cooking casserole right away, heat oven to 350°. Casserole can also be assembled, covered and refrigerated overnight before baking. Combine eggs, milk, garlic salt and white pepper in large bowl. Stir in cooked grits. Add butter and cheese, stirring until cheese melts. Stir in sausage. Spoon mixture into lightly greased 3-quart casserole. Can be refrigerated overnight. Bake, uncovered, at 350° for 1 hour or until set. Serves 8.

Chicken Gumbo

1/3 C. flour
1/3 C. melted fat or oil
1 onion, finely chopped
1 large chicken, cut into pieces
6 C. (1 1/2 qts.) hot water
Salt and pepper, as you like

Mix flour with hot fat in large pan. Cook and stir over low heat until flour is browned. (This is a "roux".) Add onion and cook until tender. Add chicken. Cook and stir until chicken is lightly browned. Add water, salt and pepper and mix well with roux. Cover pan and heat quickly to boiling. Lower heat and cook until chicken is tender. Serves 6.

Chicken Salad

- 8 C. chicken, cut up
- 1 dozen hard-boiled eggs, chopped
- 1-20 oz. can chunk pineapple, halved
- 1 medium jar green olives, chopped
- 4 oz. dry roasted almonds, chopped
- 1 bunch celery, chopped
- 3/4 C. seedless grapes, halved
- Mayonnaise

Mix all together, using enough mayonnaise to hold it together. Mix well and if possible let stand for 24 hours. To stretch for more servings, soften one package Knox gelatin in 1/4 cup cold water and mix with 1 or 2 cups chicken broth and add to above.
VARIATION: Turkey may be used instead of chicken.
NOTE: Use two (2 1/2 lb.) fryers to make 8 cups. To improve flavor, boil chicken with two chicken bouillon cubes. Salt as desired.

Chicken Scrapple

4 C. (1 qt.) chicken broth
1 1/3 C. cornmeal
1 T. flour
1 1/4 tsp. salt
1/4 tsp. poultry seasoning
2 1/2 C. finely ground cooked or canned chicken

Heat 2 cups broth in large pan. Mix cornmeal, flour, salt and poultry seasoning. Mix with unheated broth. Slowly stir cornmeal mixture into hot broth. Cook and stir until mixture thickens. Cover and cook slowly for 15 minutes longer, stirring as needed to keep from sticking. Add chicken. Cook and stir a few minutes longer. Pour into well greased loaf pan. Chill until firm. Remove from pan and cut into slices. Roll in flour. Put in heated, greased frypan and brown on both sides. Serves 6.

FOR PORK SCRAPPLE: Use 1 quart (4 cups) water or meat stock in place of chicken broth; use about 2 cups cooked or canned pork in place of chicken.

Fresh Crackling

Cut fat off of any fresh uncooked pork (ham or roast). Cut fat into very small cubes. Fry it over low heat until fat has rendered, and the cracklings are golden brown. Do not burn.

African Chicken Stew

8 chicken thighs or legs
1/8 tsp. salt
1/8 tsp. pepper
2 medium sweet potatoes
2 tsp. minced garlic
1 tsp. chili powder

1-14 1/2 oz. can diced tomatoes with garlic and onions
1 C. frozen peas
1/3 C. reduced-fat peanut butter
1/2 C. water
1 T. lemon juice

Season chicken with salt and pepper. Put in nonstick skillet over medium heat and cook 3 minutes until brown. Peel sweet potatoes and cut in bite-size pieces. Sprinkle chicken with chili and garlic. Turn and cook 3 minutes more. Remove from skillet and put potatoes and tomatoes in skillet. Put chicken on top. Bring to a boil. Cover and reduce heat and cook 10 minutes or until potatoes and chicken are done. With slotted spoon, put chicken on platter and cover with foil. Add rest of ingredients to skillet. Stir until blended and hot. Pour over chicken on skillet. Serves 4.

Desserts

Fried Apples

2 T. bacon fat or butter
Apples (2 medium apples equal 1 serving), cored, quartered and sliced, but not peeled

1/2 C. sugar

Melt fat in a skillet over low heat. Add the apples. Cover the skillet and cook gently for 5 minutes or until the apples are very juicy. Turn the apples over and sprinkle them with 1/4 cup of sugar. Cover and lower heat. Cook about 2 minutes more or until sugar is absorbed and apples are a delicate brown on the bottom. Sprinkle 1/4 cup sugar on apples and remove from pan. Serve hot.

What finer breakfast then sausage and eggs, fried apples and lots of hot, black coffee!

Souse-Congealed Pork

4 to 6 pigs feet
1/3 C. vinegar
3 red peppers, crushed

1 T. black pepper
2 T. unflavored gelatin

Boil the pigs feet in water to cover until the meat is very tender, 4 hours or more. Pick all the meat from the bones and chip it up. Mix with 4 cups of liquid it was cooked in. Add vinegar, red peppers and black pepper. Dissolve gelatin in 1/4 cup of water and add to mixture. Heat and stir until gelatin is dissolved. Pour mixture in a mold and let it jell in refrigerator. Slice and serve on wheat or rye crackers.

Sis. Charlotte Weldon's, P.G.W.M. Lemon Cake

1 box lemon cake mix
4 eggs
3/4 C. water
1 box instant lemon pudding
3/4 C. oil

TOPPING:
2 C. powdered sugar
2 T. oil
1/3 C. orange juice

Mix all ingredients, except topping, for 10 minutes. Bake at 350° for 40 minutes.
TOPPING: Mix topping ingredients together. Poke holes in cake and pour topping over top of cake.

This recipe is dedicated to my grandson, Jeffrey W. Williams.

Nana's Fresh Apple Cake

3 C. all-purpose flour
1 tsp. baking soda
1/4 tsp. salt
1 tsp. cinnamon
3 eggs
2 C. sugar
1 1/2 C. vegetable oil
3 C. chopped apples

1 C. chopped walnuts
2 tsp. vanilla
BROWN SUGAR TOPPING:
1 C. light brown sugar, firmly packed
1/4 C. milk
1/2 C. (1 stick) butter

Sift together the flour, baking soda, salt and cinnamon; set aside. Beat eggs; add sugar and oil. Beat for 3 minutes. Gradually stir in sifted dry ingredients. Fold in apples, walnuts and vanilla. Pour batter into a greased and floured 10" tube pan and bake at 350° for 1 hour and 15 minutes. Pour topping over the cake as soon as it comes out of the oven. Let cool. Loosen sides, invert on a plate and then invert on another plate, topping-side up.
BROWN SUGAR TOPPING: Combine topping ingredients in a saucepan. Bring to a full boil and boil for 3 minutes. Pour over cake right out of oven.

Peach Cake

2 eggs
1 C. butter
1 1/2 C. sugar
2 C. fresh peaches
2 C. flour
2 tsp. soda

2 tsp. cocoa
1 tsp. each allspice, cinnamon and cloves
1 C. raisins
1/2 C. water
1/2 C. nuts

Cream butter and sugar. Add eggs. Mix. Heat peaches until they make their own juice and then add peaches with juice to the creamed mixture. Sift dry ingredients together. Save some flour to dredge the raisins in. Then add the remaining flour to the creamed mixture. Partially cook the raisins in water. Drain well. Then dredge with flour. Add to the cake mixture. Bake in greased 13x9" pan for 30 minutes in 350° oven. Use your own favorite frosting.

Pork And Bean Cake

MIX BY HAND:
1-16 oz. can pork and beans, drained and mashed
1-8 oz. can crushed pineapple with juice
2 C. sugar
2 C. flour
2 tsp. cinnamon
1/2 tsp. salt

2 tsp. baking soda
1 tsp. baking powder
1 C. oil
4 eggs
CREAM CHEESE FROSTING:
1 stick (1/2 C.) butter
1 tsp. vanilla
1 lb. powdered sugar
1-8 oz. pkg. cream cheese

Bake cake batter in 13x9" pan at 350° for 35 to 40 minutes.
CREAM CHEESE FROSTING: Blend frosting ingredients well with mixer and spread over cake.

Baked Bananas Flambé

4 large bananas, peeled and sliced lengthwise
1/2 C. dark brown sugar
3 T. fresh squeezed lime juice
1/2 C. light rum
1/2 tsp. ground mace
4 T. sweet butter, cut in pieces

Preheat oven to 400°. Place bananas in a buttered baking dish. Sprinkle with sugar, juice, half of the rum and the mace. Top with butter pieces. Bake for about 12 to 15 minutes, basting several times. Heat remaining rum. Pour over bananas and light with a match. Serve over French vanilla ice cream. Serves 4.

7-Up Pound Cake

3 C. sugar
3 C. cake flour
3 sticks of butter
3/4 C. 7-Up
5 eggs
Lemon flavor, to taste

Blend dry ingredients together in a large bowl. Stir in 7-Up, lemon flavor and eggs. Melt butter and stir into the above ingredients. Mix well. Pour into bundt pan. Bake at 350° for 1 hour. Let cool before removing from pan.

Sweet Potato Cake

1 pkg. yellow cake mix
2 C. mashed, cooked sweet potatoes
2/3 C. dark brown sugar
2 T. baby food apricots
1/2 tsp. nutmeg
1 tsp. cinnamon
1 1/4 tsp. mace
1/3 C. plus 2 T. sour cream
3 eggs
1/4 tsp. soda

Mix sweet potatoes, brown sugar and spices in a small bowl and beat until sugar is well mixed; add to cake in larger bowl with rest of ingredients, and beat 3 minutes at medium speed of hand mixer. Pour into greased and floured pans. Bake in 350° for 25 to 35 minutes or until top springs back when lightly touched. Remove from oven and after 5 minutes, turn out on rack and cool. Serve plain or with confectioners' sugar glaze.

Peanut Butter Pie

1-9" baked pie shell
1 C. creamy peanut butter
1/2 C. fine sugar
6 T. half and half or milk
1 C. heavy cream, whipped until stiff
Peanuts, for garnish

Cream peanut butter, sugar and milk in a large mixing bowl. Whip cream and fold into peanut butter mixture. When mixed well, pour into baked pie shell. Chill several hours. Garnish with peanuts, chopped or whole. You can use non-dairy whipped cream as a substitute for cream.
VARIATION: You may also use chunky peanut butter, if desired.

Sweet Potato Pie

3 eggs
2 C. cooked, mashed sweet potatoes
1/2 C. white or brown sugar
1 tsp. cinnamon
1/2 tsp. nutmeg
1/4 tsp. each cloves, ginger and salt
1 1/3 C. milk
1 T. vegetable shortening, melted

Beat eggs until light and fluffy. Combine with the rest of the ingredients and blend together. Pour into 9" pie crust. Bake in hot (425°) oven for 10 minutes or until center is firm.

Easy Watermelon Pie

1 can condensed milk
1 medium-size carton non-dairy whipped topping
1/4 C. lemon juice
1/4 C. watermelon squares
Graham cracker crust

Fold together milk and non-dairy whipped topping. Add lemon juice. Fold in watermelon squares. Place mixture into graham cracker crust. Chill for 2 hours.

Aunt Creola Griggs Perfect Pie Crust

4 C. flour
1 T. sugar
2 tsp. salt
1 3/4 C. Crisco (do not substitute)
1 T. vinegar
1 large egg
1/2 C. cold water

Put first three ingredients into a bowl and mix well with table fork. Add shortening and mix until crumbly. In a small bowl, beat together with fork 1/2 cup water, vinegar and egg. Combine the two mixtures, stirring until all ingredients are moistened. Divide dough into five portions and with hands, shape each portion in a flat round patty ready for rolling. Wrap each in plastic or waxed paper and chill at least 1/2 hour. When ready to use, roll pie crust, lightly floured on both sides of patty. Roll thin. This pie crust freezes well. When freezing, wrap in foil before putting in the freezer. No matter how much you handle this dough or reroll it, the crust will never be tough. Makes two 9" double-crusts and one pie shell or 20 tart shells.
NOTE: This may also be used in a microwave. Bake pie crust on high for 3 to 4 minutes. For tart shells, bake on high for about 2 minutes (for one). If doing several, bake in a circle for about 3 minutes. Timing may differ in different microwaves.

Old-Fashioned Bread Pudding

3 eggs
2 C. milk
1/2 C. sugar
1/2 tsp. cinnamon
1/4 tsp. nutmeg
Dash of salt

1/2 tsp. lemon extract
1/2 tsp. vanilla
4 C. cube, stale bread
1/3 C. raisins
1/2 C. Concord grape preserves

In medium mixing bowl, beat eggs well. Mix in milk, sugar, cinnamon, nutmeg, salt, lemon extract and vanilla. Beat with mixer to blend thoroughly. Place half the bread in a well buttered 1 1/2-quart casserole. Sprinkle with half the raisins; pour half the egg mixture over the bread. Spoon grape preserves evenly over bread. Add remaining bread and raisins. Pour remaining egg mixture overall. Bake in preheated 350° oven until puffed and brown, about 35 minutes. Serves 6.

Baked Custard

2 eggs
2 T. sugar
Dash of salt

2 C. scalded milk
1/2 tsp. vanilla
Dash of nutmeg

Preheat oven to 300°. Beat the eggs. Add the sugar and the salt. Add scalded milk, vanilla and nutmeg. Mix well. Pour in custard cups and set cups in a pan of hot water. Bake for 65 minutes. Custard is done when it will not stick to a fork. Serve with the following topping. Serves 6.
TOPPING: Brown graham cracker crumbs in a little butter and brown sugar. Sprinkle over custard.
COCONUT CUSTARD: Add 1 1/2 tablespoons of shredded coconut to baked custard recipe.

Tea Cakes

1 C. butter or margarine
1/4 tsp. salt
2 1/4 C. flour
1 1/2 C. confectioners' sugar
1/2 tsp. cinnamon
1/2 tsp. nutmeg
1 tsp. vanilla

In large bowl with electric mixer at medium speed, beat butter until light and fluffy. At low speed, blend in 1/2 cup sugar, flour, 1/2 teaspoon cinnamon, the salt and vanilla. Chill in refrigerator for 30 minutes. Preheat oven to 400°. Grease cookie sheet. Roll dough into 1" balls. Bake 9 to 10 minutes or until a golden brown. Combine remaining sugar and cinnamon. Roll hot tea cakes in this mixture. Cool. This recipe for Cinnamon Tea Cakes makes 3 1/2 dozen.

Kathryn Brownies

1 C. butter
2 C. sugar
4 eggs
4 squares chocolate
3/4 C. hot water
2 C. sifted flour

Beat butter, sugar and eggs with mixer. Beat all ingredients until creamy. Melt chocolate in hot water. Cool; add to creamed mixture. Add 2 cups sifted flour. Bake at 375° for 25 minutes.
NOTE: If desired, may add nuts to batter.

Condiments

Coleslaw Dressing

3 egg yolks
1/2 C. sugar
2 T. butter
1 T. salt
1 C. light cream
1/2 to 1 C. vinegar, according to taste
1/4 T. cayenne
3 egg whites

Mix egg yolks, sugar, butter, salt, cream, vinegar and cayenne together and beat well. Beat egg whites until stiff. Fold in. Cook in double boiler until thickened. Makes 1 quart of dressing.

Slaw Dressing

MIX TOGETHER:
1 qt. Miracle Whip
1 C. Mazola oil
1 C. tarragon vinegar
3 1/2 C. sugar
1/4 tsp. salt

Mix well and put in refrigerator to store.

Spinach Salad Dressing

MIX TOGETHER:
1 1/4 C. oil
3 1/4 C. sugar
1 tsp. salt

1/8 C. Worcestershire sauce
3 1/2 C. vinegar
3/4 C. catsup
1 small onion

Combine with bacon bits and pour over spinach salad. Makes 1/2 gallon.
NOTE: Can use dried onions.

Strawberry-Rhubarb Jam

4 C. rhubarb
4 C. sugar

1 pkg. frozen strawberries
1 pkg. strawberry jell

Cut rhubarb into small pieces. Cook rhubarb and sugar until done. Then add frozen strawberries and jell. Mix together. Put in refrigerator. Can put some in jars and seal with paraffin for later usage.

Seasoned Salt

1 C. coarse salt
1 tsp. dried thyme
1 1/2 tsp. oregano
1 1/2 tsp. garlic powder
2 tsp. paprika

1 tsp. curry powder
2 tsp. onion powder
1/4 tsp. dill weed
2 tsp. dried mustard

Mix ingredients well. Store in airtight container.

Creole Seasoning

2 T. paprika
1 1/2 tsp. garlic powder
1 tsp. dry mustard
1/2 tsp. ground cumin
2 1/2 tsp. kosher or sea salt

1 1/2 tsp. dried thyme
1 1/2 tsp. black pepper
3/4 tsp. white pepper
1/2 tsp. onion powder
1/4 tsp. cayenne pepper

Combine all ingredients. Mix well and store in airtight container can. Use 1 to 2 tablespoons in chicken or vegetable soup.

Corn Cob Jell

3 C. liquid
1 box Sure-Jell
3 C. sugar

Corn cobs plus water
Paraffin wax

Cover corn cobs with water and boil until it turns pink; strain and reserve liquid. Take 3 cups of this liquid and add Sure-Jell. Bring to a rolling boil. Add sugar to liquid mixture. Boil 2 to 3 minutes more. Then pour into jelly glasses or jars. Melt paraffin wax and pour over warm jelly. Let harden.

Pepper Jelly

1 1/2 C. chopped bell peppers
1 1/2 C. vinegar
1/2 C. jalapeno pepper, seeded and chopped
5 1/2 C. sugar
3/4 bottle Certo

Put peppers and vinegar in blender. Put pepper mixture and sugar in large pan. Boil for 2 minutes, stirring constantly. Remove from heat; add three-fourths bottle of Certo. Stir. Pour into glass jars. Cool. Cover with paraffin.

Apple Butter

Cook slowly 2 quarts peeled apple quarters in 2 quarts cider vinegar, about 2 hours. Add 1 1/2 cups sugar, 1 1/2 teaspoons cinnamon. 1/2 teaspoon cloves and 1/2 teaspoon allspice. Cook rapidly, stirring constantly to prevent scorching, until butter sheets from spoon. Pour into clean hot jars and seal. Yields approximately 1 1/2 quarts.

Wine Jelly

2 tsp. gelatin
1 1/2 C. boiling water
3 T. lemon juice
1/2 C. cold water
1 3/4 C. wine
1/4 C. sugar

Soak gelatin in cold water. Then dissolve in boiling water with sugar, wine and 1 teaspoon vanilla. Pour cold water in mold and drain. Put wine mixture in mold and place in refrigerator until ready to serve. Serves 8.

Wine Jelly

4 1/2 C. (1 3/4 lbs.) sugar
1 box Sure-Jell fruit pectin
3/4 C. water
3 C. wine*

Measure sugar; set aside. Thoroughly mix fruit pectin and water in large saucepan. Bring to a boil over high heat. Boil 1 minute, stirring constantly. Immediately add wine and sugar. Stir over medium heat, just below boiling to dissolve sugar, about 5 minutes. Remove from heat. Skim, if necessary. Quickly pour in jelly jars. Cover with 1/8" hot paraffin wax. Makes about 4 1/2 cups.
*Use champagne, rose, grape or wine of your choice.
NOTE: Use clean, washed and rinsed jelly jars.

Barbecue Sauce

1 medium onion
2 T. butter
2 T. vinegar
2 T. brown sugar
4 T. lemon juice
2 bottles catsup
3 T. Worcestershire sauce
1/2 T. mustard
1 C. water
Salt and pepper, to taste

Brown butter in frypan. Add other ingredients and simmer. In a jar or blender, mix 2 tablespoons flour with water and thicken sauce like gravy. Pour over meat. Leftover barbecue sauce is good over chicken or pork chops. It may be frozen in ice trays, flipped out and put in bags to be used as wanted.

Grandma's Apron

I don't think our kids know what an apron is. The principal use of Grandma's Apron was to protect the dress underneath, but along with that, it served as a potholder for removing hot pans from the oven. It was wonderful for drying children's tears. From the chicken coop, the apron was used for carrying eggs, fussy chicks, and sometimes half-hatched eggs to be finished in the warming oven. When company comes, those aprons were ideal hiding places for shy kids. And when the weather was cold, Grandma wrapped it around her arms. Those big old aprons wiped many a perspiring brow, bent over the hot wood stove. Chips and kindling wood were brought into the kitchen in that

apron. From the garden, it carried all sorts of vegetables and after the peas had been shelled, it carried out the hulls. In the fall, the apron was used to bring in apples that had fallen from the trees. When unexpected company drove up the road, it was surprising how much furniture that old apron could dust in a matter of seconds. When dinner was ready, Grandma walked out onto the porch, waved her apron, and the men knew it was time to come in from the fields to dinner. It will be a long time before someone invents something that will replace that "old-time apron" that served so many purposes. Send this to those who would know, the story about Grandma's apron.

Washing Clothes

Build fire in backyard to heat kettle of rain water.
Set tubs so smoke won't blow in eyes if wind is pert.
Shave one hole cake of lie soap in boiling water.
Sort things, make three piles.
1 pile white,
1 pile colored,
1 pile work britches and rags.
To make starch, stir flour in cool water to smooth,
then thin down with boiling water. Take white thinks, rub dirty spots on board, scrub hard, and boil, then rub colored, don't boil, just wrench and starch.
Take things out of kettle with broomstick handle, then wrench, and starch.
Hang old rags on fence.
Spread tea towels on grass.
Pour wrench water in flower bed.
Scrub porch with hot soapy water.
Turn tubs upside down.
Go put on clean dress and smooth hair with hair combs.
Brew cup of tea, sit and rock a spell and count your blessings.

Paste this over your washer and dryer. Next time when you think things are bleak, read it again, kiss that washing machine and dryer, and give thanks. First thing each morning, you should run and hug your washer and dryer! For you non-southerners, wrench means rinse.

Abbreviations Commonly Used

tsp. - teaspoon
T. - tablespoon
C. - cup
pt. - pint
qt. - quart
pk. peck
bu. - bushel
oz. - ounce or ounces
lb. - pound
sq. - square
min. - minute
hr. - hour
mod. - moderate or moderately
doz. - dozen

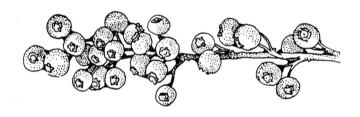

Oven Temperature

Slow (300°)
Slow moderate (325°)
Moderate (350°)
Quick moderate (375°)
Moderately hot (400°)
Hot (425°)
Very hot (475°)

Helpful Hints

Air freshener: Simmer cinnamon and clover
Ants: Red chili powder at point of entry
Car battery corrosion: Baking soda and water
Decal remover: Soak in white vinegar
Drain cleaner: Use a plunger, followed by 1/2 cup baking soda, 1/2 cup vinegar and 2 quarts of boiling water
Flea and tick repellent: scatter pine needles, fennel or rosemary on pet's bed
Flies: Well watered pot of basil
Hand cleaner for paint and grease: Baby oil
Ink spot remover: Cold water and 1 tablespoon of cream of tartar and 1 tablespoon lemon juice
Insect on plants: Soapy water on leaves, then rinse
Mildew remover: Equal parts of vinegar and salt
Oil stain remover from clothes: White chalk rubbed into stain before laundering.
Paint brush softener: Hot vinegar
Roach repellent: Chopped bay leaves and cucumber skin
Slug and snail repellent: Onion and marigold plants
Tub and tile cleaner: 1/4 cup baking soda and 1/2 cup white vinegar and warm water
Window cleaner: 1/2 cup vinegar in 1 gallon warm water

Old-Fashioned Cold Remedy

4 shots of whiskey
1 T. honey
1 tsp. butter

1 tsp. vanilla extract
Sprinkle of nutmeg, if desired

Beat and drink at bedtime. Rub chest with Vicks salve. This can be made stronger, if desired.

- DIARRHEA? Eat apples! Grate an apple with its skin, let it turn brown, and eat it to cure this condition. (Bananas are good for this ailment.)
- CLOGGED ARTERIES? Eat avocado! Mono unsaturated fat in avocados lowers cholesterol.
- HIGH BLOOD PRESSURE? Eat celery and olive oil! Olive oil has been shown to lower blood pressure. Celery contains a chemical that lowers pressure, too.
- BLOOD SUGAR IMBALANCE? Eat broccoli and peanuts! The chromium in broccoli and peanuts helps regulate insulin and blood sugar.
- KIWI: Tiny, but mighty. This is a good source of potassium, magnesium, Vitamin E and fiber. It's Vitamin C content is twice that of an orange.
- APPLE: An apple a day keeps the doctor away? Although an apple has a low Vitamin C content, it has antioxidants and flavonoids, which enhances the activity of Vitamin C thereby helping to lower the risks of colon cancer, heat attack and stroke.

- STRAWBERRY: Protective fruit. Strawberries have the highest total antioxidant power among major fruits and protects the body from cancer causing, blood vessels clogging free radicals. (Actually, any berry is good for you. They are high in antioxidants and they actually keep us young. Blueberries are the best and very versatile in the health field. They get rid of all the free-radicals that invade our bodies.)

- ORANGE: Sweetest medicine. Taking two or four oranges a day may help keep colds away, lower cholesterol, prevent and dissolve kidney stones as well as lessen the risk of colon cancer.
- WATERMELON: Coolest thirst quencher. Composed of 92% water, it is also packed with a giant dose of glutathione, which helps boost our immune system. They are also a key source of lycopene, the cancer fighting oxidant. Other nutrients found in watermelon are Vitamin C and Potassium. Watermelon also has natural substances (natural SPF sources) that keep our skin healthy, protecting our skin from those darn SUV rays.
- GUAVA AND PAPAYA: Top awards for Vitamin C. They are the clear winners for their high C content. Guava is also rich in fiber, which helps prevent constipation.
- PAPAYA: Is rich in carotene. This is good for your eyes (also good for gas and indigestion).
- TOMATOES: Are very good as a preventative measure for men, keeps those prostrate problems from invading their bodies.

- HEADACHE? Eat fish! Eat plenty of fish. Fish oil helps prevent headaches. So does ginger, which reduces inflammation and pain.
- HAY FEVER? Eat yogurt! Eat lots of yogurt before pollen season. Also, eat honey from your area (local region) daily.
- TO PREVENT STROKE. Drink tea! Prevent buildup of fatty deposits on artery walls with regular doses of tea. (Actually, tea suppresses my appetite and keeps the pounds from invading. Green tea is great for our immune system!)
- INSOMNIA (CAN'T SLEEP?): Honey! Use honey as a tranquilizer and sedative.
- ASTHMA? Eat onions! Eating onions helps ease constriction of bronchial tubes. (When I was young, my mother would make onion packs to place on our chests. This helped the respiratory ailments and actually made us breath better.)

- ARTHRITIS? Eat fish, too! Salmon, tuna, mackerel and sardines actually prevent arthritis (fish has omega oils and is good for our immune system).
- UPSET STOMACH? Bananas and ginger! Bananas will settle an upset stomach. Ginger will cure morning sickness and nausea.
- BLADDER INFECTION? Drink cranberry juice! High acid cranberry juice controls harmful bacteria.
- BONE PROBLEMS? Eat pineapple! Bone fractures and osteoporosis can be prevented by the manganese in pineapple.
- PREMENSTRUAL SYNDROME? Eat corn flakes! Women can ward off the effects of PMS with corn flakes, which help reduce depression, anxiety and fatigue.
- MEMORY PROBLEMS? Eat oysters! Oysters help improve your mental functioning by supplying much-needed zinc.
- COLDS? Eat garlic! Clear up that stuffy head with garlic (remember, garlic lowers cholesterol, too).
- COUGHING? Use red peppers! A substance similar to that found in the cough syrups is found in hot red pepper. Use red (cayenne) pepper with caution. It can irritate your tummy.
- BREAST CANCER? Eat wheat, bran and cabbage. Helps to maintain estrogen at healthy levels.
- LUNG CANCER? Eat dark green and orange and veggies! A good antidote is beta carotene, a form of Vitamin A, found in dark green and orange vegetables.
- ULCERS? Eat cabbage also! Cabbage contains chemicals that help heal both gastric and duodenal ulcers.

- Listerine therapy for toe nail fungus. Get rid of unsightly toenail fungus by soaking your toes in Listerine mouthwash. The powerful antiseptic leaves your toenails looking healthy again.
- Easy eyeglass protection. To prevent the screws in eyeglasses from loosening, apply a small drop of Maybelline Crystal Clear nail polish to the threads of the screws before tightening them.
- Coca-Cola cure for rust. Forget those expensive rust removers. Just saturate an abrasive sponge with Coca-Cola and scrub the rust stain. The phosphoric acid in the Coke is what gets the job done.
- Cleaning liquid that doubles as bug killer. If menacing bees, wasps, hornets or yellow jackets get in your home and you can't find the insecticide, try a spray of Formula 409. Insects drop to the ground instantly.
- Smart splinter remover. Just pour a drop of Elmer's GluAll over the splinter; let dry, and peel the dried glue off the skin. The splinter sticks to the dried glue.
- Hunt's tomato paste boil cure. Cover the boil with Hunt's tomato paste as a compress. The acids from the tomatoes soothe the pain and bring the boil to a head.
- Balm for broke blisters. To disinfect a broken blister, dab on a few drops of Listerine, a powerful antiseptic.
- Heinz vinegar to heal bruises. Soak a cotton ball in white vinegar and apply it to the bruise for 1 hour. The vinegar reduces the blueness and speeds up the healing process.
- Kills fleas instantly. Dawn dish washing liquid does the trick. Add a few drops to your dog's bath and shampoo the animal thoroughly. Rinse well to avoid skin irritations. Goodbye fleas.
- Rainy day cure for dog odor. Next time your dog comes in from the rain, simply wipe down the animal with Bounce or any dryer sheet, instantly making your dog smell springtime fresh.

- Eliminate ear mites. All it takes is a few drops of Wesson corn oil in your cat's ear. Massage it in and then clean with a cotton ball. Repeat daily for 3 days. The oil soothes the cat's skin, smothers the mites and accelerates healing.
- Quaker oats for fast pain relief. It's not for breakfast anymore! Mix 2 cups of Quaker oats and 1 cup of water in a bowl and warm in the microwave for 1 minute. Cool slightly. Apply the mixture to your hands for soothing relief from arthritis pain.

Bath Salts

1 box Epson salts
1 drop food coloring

15 drops essential oil per C. of salt

Pour salts into jars or containers.

Dusting Powder

2 C. cornstarch
20 drops essential oil, any fragrance

1 C. baking soda
Wooden boxes
Powder puffs

Mix cornstarch and baking soda together. Add drops of essential oils and mix. Place powder in containers.
NOTE: Give as gifts with powder puffs.

- Did you know that? Drinking two glasses of Gatorade can relieve headache pain almost immediately, without the unpleasant side effects caused by traditional "pain relievers."
- Did you know that Colgate toothpaste makes an excellent salve for burns. Before you head to the drugstore for a high-priced inhaler filled with mysterious chemicals, try chewing on a couple of curiously strong Altoids peppermints. They'll clear up your stuffed nose.
- Achy muscles from a bout of the flu? Mix 1 tablespoon of horseradish in 1 cup of olive oil. Let the mixture sit for 30 minutes, then apply it as a massage oil, for instant relief for aching muscles.
- Sore throat? Just mix 1/4 cup of vinegar with 1/4 cup of honey and take 1 tablespoon six times a day. The vinegar kills the bacteria.
- Cure urinary tract infections with Alka-Seltzer. Just dissolve two tablets in a glass of water and drink it at the onset of the symptom. Alka-Seltzer begins eliminating urinary tract infections almost instantly, even though the product was never advertised for this. (Note: Alka-Seltzer Plus cold medicine is not the same and contains aspirin, which can cause stomach bleeding, if you have ulcers.)
- Honey remedy for skin blemishes. Cover the blemish with a dab of honey and place a Band-Aid over it. Honey kills the bacteria, keeps the skin sterile, and speeds healing. Works overnight.

Clean-up Tips

Appliances: To shine chrome, use vinegar or window cleaner.

If the numbers on your oven dial are worn, take a yellow crayon and rub it all over the number on the dial. Gently wipe off the excess crayon and paint with clear nail polish.

To clean splattered food from the interior of your microwave, bring one cup of water to a boil until steam forms on the inside walls of microwave. Remove water and wipe with a damp cloth. You may have to repeat the process to get a really big job done.

To rid yellowing from white appliances try this: Mix together: 1/2 cup bleach, 1/4 cup baking soda and 4 cups warm water. Apply with a sponge and let set for 10 minutes. Rinse and dry thoroughly.

Instead of using commercial waxes, shine with rubbing alcohol.

For quick clean-ups, rub with equal parts of water and household ammonia.

Or, try club soda. It cleans and polishes at the same time.

Blender: Fill part way with hot water and add a drop of detergent. Cover and turn it on for a few seconds. Rinse and drain dry.

Burnt and scorched pans: Sprinkle burnt pans liberally with baking soda, adding just enough water to moisten. Let stand for several hours. You can generally lift the burned portions right out of the pan.

Stubborn stains on non-stick cookware can be removed by boiling 2 tablespoons of baking soda, 1/2 cup vinegar and 1 cup water for 10 minutes. Re-season pan with salad oil.

Cast-iron skillets: Clean the outside of the pan with commercial oven cleaner. Let set for 2 hours and the accumulated black stains can be removed with vinegar and water.

Dishwasher: Run a cup of white vinegar through the entire cycle in an empty dishwasher to remove all soap film.

Clogged drains: When a drain is clogged with grease, pour a cup of salt and a cup of baking soda into the drain followed by a kettle of boiling water. The grease will usually dissolve immediately and open the drain.

Coffee grounds are a no-no. They do a nice job of clogging, especially if they get mixed with grease.

Dusting: Spray furniture polish on the bristles of your broom and the dust and dirt will be easier to collect when you sweep.

Dish Drainer: Remove hard water stains from your dish drainer by tilting the low end of the board slightly and pouring one cup of white vinegar over the board. Let it set overnight and rub off with a sponge in the morning.

Glassware: Never put a delicate glass in hot water bottom side first; it will crack from sudden expansion. The most delicate glassware will be safe if it is slipped in edgewise.

Vinegar is a must when washing crystal. Rinse in 1 part vinegar to 3 parts warm water. Air dry.

When one glass is tucked inside another, do not force them apart. Fill the top glass with cold water and dip the lower one in hot water. They will come apart without breaking.

Grater: For a fast and simple clean-up, rub salad oil on the grater before using.

Use a toothbrush to brush lemon rind, cheese, onion or whatever out of the grater before washing.

Thermos bottle: Fill the bottle with warm water, add 1 teaspoon of baking soda and allow to soak.

Oven: Following a spill, sprinkle with salt immediately. When oven is cool, brush off burnt food and wipe with a damp sponge.

Sprinkle bottom of oven with automatic dishwasher soap and cover with wet paper towels. Let stand for a few hours.

A quick way to clean oven parts is to place a bath towel in the bathtub and pile all removable parts from the oven onto it. Draw enough hot water to just cover the parts and sprinkle a cup of dishwasher soap over it. While you are cleaning the inside of the oven, the rest will be cleaning itself.

An inexpensive oven cleaner: Set oven on warm for about 20 minutes, then turn off. Place a small dish of full strength ammonia on the top shelf. Put a large pan of boiling water on the bottom shelf and let it set overnight. In the morning, open oven and let it air a while before washing off with soap and water. Even the hard baked-on grease will wash off easily.

Plastic cups, dishes and containers: Coffee or tea stains can be scoured with baking soda. Or, fill the stained cup with hot water and drop in a few denture cleanser tablets. Let soak for 1 hour.

To rid foul odors from plastic containers, place crumpled-up newspaper (black and white only) into the container. Cover tightly and leave overnight.

Refrigerator: To help eliminate odors fill a small bowl with charcoal (the kind used for potted plants) and place it on a shelf in the refrigerator. It absorbs odors rapidly.

An open box of baking soda will absorb food odors for at least a month or two.

A little vanilla poured on a piece of cotton and placed in the refrigerator will eliminate odors.

To prevent mildew from forming, wipe with vinegar. The acid effectively kills the mildew fungus. Use a glycerin soaked cloth to wipe sides and shelves. Future spills wipe up easily. And after the freezer has been defrosted, coat the inside coils with glycerin. The next time you defrost, the ice will loosen quickly and drop off in sheets.

Wash inside and out with a mixture of 3 tablespoons of baking soda in a quart of warm water.

Sinks: For a sparkling white sink, place paper towels across the bottom of your sink and saturate with household bleach. Let set for 1/2 hour or so.

Rub stainless steel sinks with lighter fluid if rust marks appear. After the rust disappears wipe with your regular kitchen cleanser.

Use a cloth dampened with rubbing alcohol to remove water spots from stainless steel.

Spots on stainless steel can also be removed with white vinegar.

Club soda will shine up stainless steel sinks in a jiffy.

Teakettle: To remove lime deposits, fill with equal parts of vinegar and water. Bring to a boil and allow to stand overnight.

To unplug sink: Pour in one cup or more of white vinegar and a cup of baking soda, then add hot water out of the tap at full force. When bubbling stops, drain should be clear. Need no plumber.

Fingerprints off the kitchen door and walls: Take away fingerprints. Spot removal: Two parts water and one part rubbing alcohol are the basic ingredients in any commercial spot remover.

Keeping Furniture Clean

To remove polish build-up: Mix 1/2 cup vinegar and 1/2 cup water. Rub with a soft cloth that has been moistened with solution, but wrung out. Dry immediately with another soft cloth.

Polishing carved furniture: Dip an old soft toothbrush into furniture polish and brush lightly. Cigarette burns: For small minor burns, try rubbing mayonnaise into the burn. Let set for a while before wiping off with a soft cloth.

Burns can be repaired with a wax stick (available in all colors at paint and hardware stores). Gently scrape away the charred finish. Heat a knife blade and melt the shellac stick against the heated blade. Smooth over damaged area with your finger. But always consider the value of the furniture. It might be better to have a professional make the repair.

Or, make a paste of rottenstone (available at hardware stores) and salad oil. Rub into the burned spot only, following the grain of wood. Wipe clean with a cloth that has been dampened in oil. Wipe dry and apply your favorite furniture polish.

Removing paper that is stuck to a wood surface: Do not scrape with a knife. Pour any salad oil, a few drops at a time, on the paper. Let set for a while and rub with a soft cloth. Repeat the procedure until the paper is completely gone.

Old decals can be removed easily by painting them with several coats of rub with the grain of the wood when repairing a scratch.

Walnut: Remove the meat from a fresh, unsalted walnut or pecan nut. Break it in half and rub the scratch with the broken side of the nut.

Mahogany: You can either rub the scratch with a dark brown crayon or buff with brown paste wax.

Red Mahogany: Apply ordinary iodine with a number 0 artist's brush.

Maple: Combine equal amounts of iodine and denatured alcohol. Apply with a Q-tip, then dry, wax and buff.

Ebony: Use black shoe polish, black eyebrow pencil or black crayon.

Teakwood: Rub very gently with 0000 steel wool. Rub in equal amounts of linseed oil and turpentine.

Light-finished furniture: Scratches can be hidden by using tan shoe polish. However, only on shiny finishes.

For all minor scratches: Cover each scratch with a generous amount of white petroleum jelly. Allow it to remain on for 24 hours. Rub into wood. Remove excess and polish as usual.

For larger scratches: Fill by rubbing with a wax stick (available in all colors at your hardware or paint store) or a crayon that matches the finish of the wood.

Three solutions to remove white water rings and spots: Dampen a soft cloth with water and put a dab of toothpaste on it. For stubborn stains, add baking soda to the toothpaste.

Make a paste of butter or mayonnaise and cigarette ashes. Apply to spot and buff away.

Apply a paste of salad oil and salt. Let stand briefly. Wipe and polish.

Marble table-top stains: Sprinkle salt on a fresh-cut lemon. Rub very lightly over stain. Do not rub hard or you will ruin the polished surface. Wash off with soap and water.

Scour with a water and baking soda paste. Let stand for a few minutes before rinsing with warm water.

Removing candle wax from wooden finishes: Soften the wax with a hair dryer. Remove wax with paper toweling and wash down with a solution of vinegar and water.

Plastic table tops: You will find that a coat of Turtle Wax is a quick pick-up for dulled plastic table tops and counters.

Or, rub in toothpaste and buff.

Glass table tops: Rub in a little lemon juice. Dry with paper towels and shine with newspaper for a sparkling table.

Toothpaste will remove small scratches from glass.

Chrome cleaning: For sparkling clean chrome without streaks, use a cloth dampened in ammonia.

Removing glue: Cement glue can be removed by rubbing with cold cream, peanut butter or salad oil.

Wicker: Wicker needs moisture, so use a humidifier in the winter. To prevent drying out, apply lemon oil occasionally.

Never let wicker freeze. This will cause cracking and splitting.

Wash with a solution of warm salt water to keep from turning yellow.

Metal furniture: To remove rust, a good scrubbing with turpentine should accomplish this job.

Vinyl upholstery: Never oil vinyl as this will make it hard. It is almost impossible to soften again. For proper cleaning, sprinkle baking soda or vinegar on a rough, damp cloth, then wash with a mild dishwashing soap.

Soiled upholstery: Rub soiled cotton upholstery fabric with an artgum eraser or squares (purchased at stationery store).

Leather upholstery: Prevent leather from cracking by polishing regularly with a cream made of 1 part vinegar and 2 parts linseed oil. Clean with a damp cloth and saddle soap.

Grease stains: Absorb grease on furniture by pouring salt on the spill immediately.

Laundry Care

Spot removal: Two parts water and one part rubbing alcohol are the basic ingredients in any commercial spot remover.

Clean machine: Fill your washer with warm water and add a gallon of distilled vinegar. Run the machine through the entire cycle to unclog and clean soap scum from hoses.

Too sudsy: When your washer overflows with too many suds, sprinkle salt in the water - the suds will disappear.

Hand-washed sweaters: Add a capful of hair cream rinse to the final rinse water when washing sweaters.

Whiter fabric: Linen or cotton can be whitened by boiling in a mixture or 1 part cream of tartar and 3 parts water.

Whitest socks: Boil socks in water to which a lemon slice has been added.

Freshen feather pillows: Put feather pillows in the dryer and tumble, then air outside.

Lintless corduroy: While corduroy is still damp, brush with clothes brush to remove all lint.

Ironing tip: When pressing pants, iron the top part on the wrong side. Iron the legs on the right side. This gives the pockets and waistband a smooth look.

Creaseless garments: Take an empty cardboard paper towel roll and cut through it lengthwise. Slip it over a wire hanger to prevent a crease from forming in the garment to be hung on the hanger.

Remove creases from hems: Sponge material with a white vinegar solution and press flat to remove creases in hems.

Bedroom ironing: A good place to iron is in the bedroom. Closets are nearby to hang clothes up immediately, and the bed makes a good surface on which to fold clothes and separate items into piles.

Ironing board cover: When washing your ironing board cover, attach it to the board while it is still damp. When it dries, the surface will be completely smooth. Starch your ironing board cover. This helps the cover stay clean longer.

Lint remover: Add a yard of nylon netting to your dryer with the wet clothes - it will catch most of the lint.

Washer advice: Button all buttons on clothing and turn inside out before putting into the washer. Fewer buttons will fall off and garments will fade less if turned inside out.

Soiled collars: Use a small paintbrush and brush hair shampoo into soiled shirt collars before laundering. Shampoo is made to dissolve body oils.

Faster ironing: Place a strip of heavy-duty aluminum foil over the entire length of the ironing board and cover with pad. As you iron, heat will reflect through the underside of the garment.

Ironing embroidery: Lay the embroidery piece upside-down on a Turkish towel before ironing. All the little spaces between the embroidery will be smooth when you are finished.

Removing Stains from Washables

Alcoholic beverages: Pre-soak or sponge fresh stains immediately with cold water, then with cold water and glycerin. Rinse with vinegar for a few seconds if stain remains. These stains may turn brown with age. If wine stain remains, rub with concentrated detergent; wait 15 minutes; rinse. Repeat if necessary. Wash with detergent in hottest water safe for fabric.
Baby Food: Use liquid laundry detergent and brush into stain with an old toothbrush then wash.
Blood: Pre-soak in cold or warm water at least 30 minutes. If stain remains, soak in lukewarm ammonia water (3 tablespoons per gallon water). Rinse. If stain remains, work in detergent, and wash, using bleach safe for fabric.
Candle wax: Use a dull knife to scrape off as much as possible. Place fabric between 2 blotters or facial tissues and press with warm iron. Remove color stain with non-flammable dry cleaning solvent. Wash with detergent in the hottest water safe for fabric.
Chewing gum: Rub area with ice, then scrape off with a dull blade. Sponge with dry cleaning solvent; allow to air dry. Wash in detergent and hottest water safe for fabric.
Cosmetics: Loosen stain with a non-flammable dry cleaning solvent. Rub detergent in until stain outline is gone. Wash in hottest water and detergent safe for fabric.
Deodorants: Sponge area with white vinegar. If stain remains, soak with denatured alcohol. Wash with detergent in hottest water safe for fabric.

Dye: If dye transfers from a noncolorfast item during washing, immediately bleach discolored items. Repeat as necessary BEFORE drying. On whites use color remover. CAUTION: Do not use color remover in washer, or around washer and dryer as it may damage the finish.
Fruit and fruit juices: Sponge with cold water. Pre-soak in cold or warm water for at least 30 minutes. Wash with detergent and bleach safe for fabric.
Grass: Pre-soak in cold water for at least 30 minutes. Rinse. Pretreat with detergent, hot water, and bleach safe for fabric. On acetate and colored fabrics, use 1 part of alcohol to 2 parts water.
Grease, oil, tar or butter: Method 1: Use powder or chalk absorbents to remove as much grease as possible. Pre-treat with detergent or non-flammable dry cleaning solvent, or liquid shampoo. Wash in hottest water safe for fabric, using plenty of detergent.
Method 2: Rub spot with lard and sponge with a non-flammable dry cleaning solvent. Wash in hottest water and detergent safe for fabric.
Perspiration: Sponge fresh stain with ammonia; old stain with vinegar. Pre-soak in cold or warm water. Rinse. Wash in hottest water safe for fabric. If fabric is yellowed, use bleach. If stain still remains, dampen and sprinkle with meat tenderizer, or pepsin. Let stand 1 hour. Brush off and wash. For persistent odor, sponge with colorless mouthwash.

Removing Stains from Carpets & Floors

Candle drippings: For spilled wax on carpet, use a brown paper bag as a blotter and run a hot iron over it, which will absorb the wax.

Dog stains: Blot up excess moisture with paper towel. Pour club soda on the spot and continue blotting. Lay a towel over the spot and set a heavy object on top in order to absorb all the moisture.

Rug care: When washing and drying foam-backed throw rugs, never wash in hot water, and use the "air only" dryer setting to dry. Heat will ruin foam.

Cleaning rugs: If the rug is only slightly dirty, you can clean it with cornmeal. Use a stiff brush to work the cornmeal into the pile of the rug. Take it all out with the vacuum.

Spills on the rug: When spills happen, go to the bathroom and grab a can of shaving cream. Squirt it on the spot then rinse off with water.

Ballpoint ink marks: Saturate the spots with hairspray. Allow to dry. Brush lightly with a solution of water and vinegar.

Glue: Glue can be loosened by saturating the spot with a cloth soaked in vinegar.

Repairing braided rugs: Braided rugs often rip apart. Instead of sewing them, use clear fabric glue to repair. It's that fast and easy.

Repairing a burn: Remove some fuzz from the carpet, either by shaving or pulling out with a tweezer. Roll into the shape of the burn. Apply a good cement glue to the backing of the rug and press the fuzz down into the burned spot. Cover with a piece of cleansing tissue and place a heavy book on top. This will cause the glue to dry very slowly and will get the best results.

Spot remover for outdoor carpeting: Spray spots liberally with a pre-wash commercial spray. Let it set several minutes, then hose down and watch the spots disappear.

Blood on the rug: When you get blood on your rug, rub off as much as you can at first, then take a cloth soaked in cold water and wet the spot, wiping it up as you go. If a little bit remains, pour some ammonia onto the cool, wet cloth and lightly wipe that over the spot, too. Rinse it right away with cold water.

Crayon Marks: Use silver polish to remove from vinyl tile or linoleum.

Spilled nail polish: Allow to almost dry, then peel off of waxed floors or tile.

Tar spots: Use paste wax to remove tar from floors. Works on shoes, too.

Dusting floors: Stretch a nylon stocking over the dust mop. After using, discard the stocking and you will have a clean mop.

Varnished floors: Use cold tea to clean woodwork and varnished floors.

Spilled grease: Rub floor with ice cubes to solidify grease. Scrape up excess and wash with soapy water.

Quick shine: Put a piece of waxed paper under your dust mop. Dirt will stick to the mop and the wax will shine your floors.

Unmarred floors: Put thick old socks over the legs of heavy furniture when moving across floors.

Wood floor care: Never use water or water-based cleaners on wood floors. Over a period of time, warping and swelling will develop.

Heel marks: Just take a pencil eraser and wipe them off.

Floor polisher: When cleaning the felt pads of your floor polisher, place the pads between layers of newspaper and press with an iron to absorb built-up wax.

Garage floors: In an area where a large amount of oil has spilled, lay several thicknesses of newspaper. Saturate the paper with water; press flat against the floor. When dry, remove the newspaper and the spots will have disappeared.

Basement floors: Sprinkle sand on oily spots, let it absorb the oil, and sweep up.

NOTES

NOTES

NOTES

NOTES

To Order Copies

Please send me _____ copies of ***The Green, Grits, & Hoecakes Cookbook*** at $9.95 each plus $3.00 S/H. (Make checks payable to Hearts 'N Tummies.)

Name _____

Street _____

City _____ State _____ Zip _____

QUIXOTE PRESS
3544 Blakslee Street
Wever IA 52658
1-800-571-2665

To Order Copies

Please send me _____ copies of ***The Green, Grits, & Hoecakes Cookbook*** at $9.95 each plus $3.00 S/H. (Make checks payable to Hearts 'N Tummies.)

Name _____

Street _____

City _____ State _____ Zip _____

QUIXOTE PRESS
3544 Blakslee Street
Wever IA 52658
1-800-571-2665